The
effective
change
ma

The Cha[...
Body of

SECOND EDI[...

© 2014 Change Management Institute

Published by VIVID Publishing (POD Edition)
P.O. Box 948, Fremantle
Western Australia 6959
www.vividpublishing.com.au

National Library of Australia Cataloguing-in-Publication data:
Title: The Effective Change Manager : The change management body of knowledge /
             The Change Management Institute.
ISBN: 978-1-925171-02-0 (paperback)
Subjects: Organizational change--Management.
             Executive ability.
             Management.
             Leadership.
Other Authors/Contributors:
             The Change Management Institute.
Dewey Number: 658.406

The mission of the Change Management Institute (CMI) is to promote excellence in the management of change by setting standards, educating and supporting change management practitioners and organizations and promoting the value of change management.

We are an independent professional organization that is uniquely positioned to advance the interests of change management. Since 2005, CMI has been providing opportunities for change management professionals to build knowledge and skills and network with other professionals.

We provide:

- **Education** – developing the capability of change practitioners
- **Networking** – hosting a range of networking opportunities
- **Accreditation** – developing standards and recognizing excellence in the management of change

As a member-owned organization we focus on delivering real benefits to our members and offer:

- **Credibility** – membership and affiliation to a professional industry organization
- **Capability** – access to professional development opportunities
- **Connection** – local connection within a global community
- **Discounts** – special member prices on events and benefits

Our organization is built upon the support and effort of our incredible volunteers. We truly are members supporting members and offer a strong peer network of change professionals. We hope that you will become part of CMI and support the evolution of the change management industry together with us.

 Change Management Institute

www.change-management-institute.com

Design: Wills Brand Design, Sydney

Concept for original graphics from David King, Systemic Limited

Foreword

I am delighted to introduce you to the first official and independent Change Management Body of Knowledge (CMBoK) for the Change Management profession. Our members and stakeholders told us the time had come to define the knowledge that our profession relies on. Newcomers to change management told us they needed a reliable and independent single source of truth to guide their professional development. To experienced practitioners this feels like a 'coming of age' for change management.

The feedback we have had on this first edition is encouraging. There were comments such as:

'[The CMBoK]... strikes a good balance between being professional, theoretical and credible with being accessible, understandable and practical for practicing or aspiring professionals'

'I thoroughly enjoyed reading this content. It is well written, gave me some timely reminders about the varied aspects of an effective Change Manager's work and inspired me to seek out some new readings.'

'Very, very impressive!'

Now we want to hear from you. As with all our standards, this one has been carefully developed and tested over a long period involving a wide range of stakeholders. We know our profession is still growing so it is constantly open for feedback and we'd love to hear what you think. Tell us if we've missed something or if you have a great book or article that you refer to frequently so we can share this information with your colleagues across the profession and across the world.

Finally I would like to add a personal thank you to the team involved in writing, managing and reviewing this incredible resource. Creating it has been a three-year journey for CMI and it would not be in your hands now without the hard work (most of it unpaid) of a group of dedicated people.

Now turn the page and enjoy! I guarantee you'll learn something. I did.

Caroline Perkins
President, Change Management Institute

Introduction

Change Management has its roots in the second half of the 20th Century. Changes in social and organizational structures, frequently driven by changing technology, created an environment of rapid and discontinuous change. Business leaders, managers and professionals from a range of disciplines recognized the challenge of creating and sustaining value in this challenging environment. It became a commonplace observation that change in organizations frequently became chaotic; it destroyed value, rather than creating it.

Organization Development practitioners and academics approached change from the perspective of psychological and social disciplines. Half a century of social science research was plundered to gather insights that might help organizations to engage people more effectively in the change process. The human side of change became a key driver of success.

Project and Programme Management professionals, drawing on operational research and other well-developed academic disciplines approached change from a different perspective. Their fast-developing profession provided powerful tools to define, plan and control change initiatives in organizations. They offered structures and processes that reassured organizations that change could be managed.

Systems theory, chaos theory and other powerful strands of thought also made their contributions to understanding change and shaping the way it is managed. Large consulting firms began assigning their most capable practitioners to support organizations approaching significant changes. The literature of Change Management became more and more prominent in business and universities began to offer courses dedicated to Change Management.

From these diverse professional backgrounds, a number of individuals began to define themselves as Change Specialists or Change Managers. Organizations, struggling to maintain or increase value through times of change started to employ people in roles identified as 'Change Manager', either internally or through external recruitment processes. Consultants advertised their Change Management services and were engaged to provide guidance. The discipline of Change Management began to form.

Change Management is an **emerging** profession

Change Management is an interdisciplinary profession

There is a substantial and growing body of literature about organizational change. However, it is clear that effective Change Management draws on the expertise of a wide range of other professional disciplines. The history of Change Management illustrates some of the disciplines that contribute to the effective management of organizational change. In this Change Management Body of Knowledge (CMBoK) we have sought to identify, recognize and calibrate those elements on which the Change Management profession relies.

The specific context of any change initiative or process will determine which of these elements are most significant. That context includes the national, ethnic and organizational cultures in which the change takes place. It also includes the particular nature of the change and the forces that are driving – and resisting – it. It certainly includes the people involved, especially those leading the change process, and the outcomes that are required.

Because of this variation in the context, no single definition of the knowledge required to underpin effective Change Management will meet with universal approval. Professionals with different orientations, from different cultures and facing different challenges will (unsurprisingly) reach different conclusions about the 'correct' content of a CMBoK.

In this edition we have built on eight years of Change Management Institute research which has defined what effective Change Managers actually *do*. This research has drawn on the experience of more than six hundred Change Management professionals in thirty countries, and is published as a competence framework for a Change Management practitioner (www. change-management-institute.com).

In developing this CMBoK we have engaged in further research with a similarly global constituency to define and balance ideas about what Change Managers must know in order to display those competences effectively – and to deliver change successfully. Our decisions about what to include, and with what emphasis, will not please everyone – but the results are based on strong global foundations. We believe it to be a worthwhile contribution to defining this emergent profession.

The Change Management profession is no longer embryonic and is readily identifiable in organizational, and especially in business literature. Nor is Change Management in its infancy. Early faltering footsteps and hesitant speech have given way to a sense of balance about the profession and to a clear voice that articulates a strong contribution to thought leadership. Perhaps, however, we could say that Change Management is in its adolescence. It is no longer dependent on its parent disciplines – such as organization development and project management – and is becoming 'its own person'. Parental influences are still strong, but it is now making substantial and distinctive contributions to the world around.

However, the Change Management profession is itself in a state of rapid change and growth. Our research shows that the numbers of explicitly Change Management jobs is growing, and more organizations are actively seeking to build Change Management capacity and capability. The shapes of these initiatives are many and varied; the knowledge and competence of the effective Change Manager still needs to evolve to meet the resulting demands. New ideas and innovative approaches –spread by online forums faster than printed literature can keep up – are rushing around the globe and are driving behaviour which varies from thoughtful and highly sophisticated to reflexive and faddish.

This is a good time to identify the best in the developing Change Management profession. We have taken an 'agile' approach in the CMBoK. We have chosen not to wait until all is clear and the evidence is universally agreed. This first edition is a work in progress. As we publish we are already gathering data and insights from the global Change Management community, which will shape the second edition. Through this iterative process we aim to maintain a clear, current, convenient and valuable reference to what organizations require of an effective Change Manager.

Change Management is a **developing** profession

What is a 'Body of Knowledge'?

Change Management knowledge that underpins effective practice

A 'Body of Knowledge' is a document produced by a professional association to describe and define the knowledge that underpins effective practice in a trade or profession.

The CMBoK:

- Identifies the Knowledge Areas required to practise effectively as a Change Manager across a range of situations;

- Provides definitions and descriptions of each of these Knowledge Areas, including a clear indication of the depth of knowledge required in each area;

- Shows how areas of knowledge relate to one another, and to their practical application in the Change Management Institute competence model; and

- Offers a reliable, reputable and realistic range of reference sources in which these Knowledge Areas can be found and studied.

PURPOSE

A Body of Knowledge for Change Management that provides a firm foundation for organizations, practitioners, authors and academics

This CMBoK is designed for practitioners, employers, authors and academics. It provides:

- Practising Change Managers – or those aspiring to practise as Change Managers – with a recognized outline of the required knowledge (for those seeking accreditation through the Change Management Institute's professional accreditation scheme it describes the knowledge applicants must display in their work);

- People employing Change Managers (or contracting for Change Management services) with a description of the areas of expertise they can reasonably expect of an applicant; and

- Authors and academics with well-researched information on which to base books and courses.

THE CMI CHANGE MANAGEMENT MATURITY MODEL AND THE CMBOK

The CMI Organisational Change Maturity Model outlines three levels of maturity in our discipline:

- **Project** change management
- **Business** change readiness, and
- **Organizational** change leadership.

The table at Appendix A (see page 186) summarises how this guide relates to all three maturity levels.

In response to feedback from members we have focused this first edition of the CMBoK on project change management and the role of the Change Manager as outlined in our Change Management Practitioner Competency Model. Where it is relevant we have made reference to concepts from the organizational and business domains (such as Change Management Offices, emergent change and change leadership) but not covered them in detail.

As the body of knowledge develops we expect to incorporate the feedback we receive to expand on the specific knowledge underpinning practice in the business and across the organization.

THE CMI CMBOK IN CONTEXT

Practitioners from across the world have developed CMI's independent Change Management standards and these have been in use for several years. They include two models:

- The Change Management Practitioner Competency Model (issued in 2008, updated in 2010 and 2012) defines what a practitioner does; and

- The Organisational Change Management Maturity Model (issued in 2012) outlines what a mature organization does.

Information about both models can be downloaded from:

https://www.change-management-institute.com/tools-models

The CMBoK describes the knowledge that underpins Change Management practice across both domains.

> The CMBoK supports the project level of the CMI Organisational Change Management Maturity Model

> The CMBoK complements the Practitioner Competency Model and the Organisational Maturity Model

PRACTITIONER ACCREDITATION

CMI offers accreditation of Change Management practitioners against a well-established global benchmark. Accreditation provides colleagues and employers with an independent validation of a practitioner's ability to perform a Change Management role effectively. The accreditation scheme was developed in response to an ongoing call from practitioners for a high quality, robust and reliable assessment process to recognize excellence in the management of change. Those that have been awarded their accreditation tell us it creates a greater respect for them and the profession and it helps them to stand out from the crowd when applying for new roles. Employers tell us how relieved they are to have an independent assessment of a candidate's workplace performance to rely on.

Practitioners with typically three or more years' experience aim for the ACM (Accredited Change Manager). The benchmark standard used is the CMI Change Management Practitioner Competency Model. The assessment process involves both a written and face to face assessment, as well as reference checks.

Less experienced practitioners (typically with one to three years' experience) aim for our foundation level accreditation. They provide evidence of Change Management knowledge (based on this CMBoK) as well as examples of their experience in a novice level Change Management role.

Go to the CMI website to find more about accreditation.

www.change-management-institute.com/accreditation

THIS IS JUST THE BEGINNING

Our profession is built on a foundation of consultation and this has been demonstrated in the way the CMBoK has been developed. The content reflects the views of CMI members and stakeholders over a three year period from 2010 to 2013.

Our profession is constantly developing and this is reflected in the way we manage this body of knowledge. We see it as a constant 'work in progress' always being updated with feedback from our community. In line with this, and the approach we take with all our standards, the CMBoK is always open for feedback and will be updated regularly. As this is the first issue we anticipate an update towards the end of 2014, then another every two years after that. Keep an eye on the CMI website for deadlines!

You can provide input at any time and there are two ways to do this:

1. Complete the short 10 minute survey on the CMI website (available at: https://www.change-management-institute.com/cmbok); and

2. Send us an email at cmbok@change-management-institute.com. Please provide the relevant page and section references so that we can use the feedback you provide. If you would like to see specific literature references included please provide full details following the format used in this document.

The CMBoK reflects a developing profession and is a constant 'work in progress' that will be updated regularly

Acknowledgements

The CMBoK is a collaboration between CMI and the APMG and is a product of the effort, enthusiasm and dedication of a team of expert leads, authors and reviewers

CMI would like to thank APMG for the partnership and support demonstrated throughout this project. Given CMI's independent status the decision to partner with another organization was not taken lightly and involved several months of negotiation. We have been delighted with the cooperation and collaboration demonstrated between the two organizations throughout.

Believers

The global Change Management community would like to recognize the vision, energy and determination of the leaders of both organizations in taking this from a good idea to a valuable contribution to the global practice of Change Management.

Caroline Perkins (CMI), Richard Pharro & Keith Williams (APMG)

Authors

CMI would like to recognize the authors of the document who worked tirelessly to turn everyone's contributions and suggestions into a valuable coherent reference.

Dan Skelsey, David King, Ranjit Sidhu, Richard Smith

The authoring team appreciates the consistent support of their work given by Gavin Webb (APMG).

CMBoK Leads

CMI would like to recognize the contribution of the CMBoK Leads who set the tone for the collaborative development and delivered a quality product to a seemingly impossible deadline.

Helen Campbell ACM (CMI), Richard Smith (APMG)

Review Panel

CMI knew that Change Managers were keen to get their hands on this first edition, so we used the data from three years of consultation to develop an initial draft. Then we asked all those responding to the CMBoK survey "Who would you trust to review the first draft of the CMBoK on your behalf?" The responses drove the composition of the review panel with reviewers coming from the UK, the USA, from Europe, Australasia and China. The panel included academics, practitioners and Change Management experts as well as CMI Board members, CMI Country Leads and CMI Accredited Change Managers (ACMs).

This CMBoK, like every other CMI initiative, is the product of many hours of hard work given freely by volunteers. While this document is the product of many people's input CMI particularly recognizes the significant contribution, and many hours of work invested in the review, by the following people:

Arnab Banerjee	Dr Elizabeth Short	Dr Janet Cole
Bithika O'Dwyer	David Miller	Jo Millott
Caroline Perkins ACM	Emma Hansford ACM	Melanie Franklin ACM
Chantal Patruno	Fran Leys ACM	Nicola Busby
Chris Bayley ACM	Gillian Perry ACM	Patrick Mayfield
Chris Macdonald	Helen Campbell ACM	Phil Angell
Dr Christina Kirsch	Ira Blake ACM	Tanja van den Akker
Clare Ellis	Jane Judd	

Editorial and practical information about the CMBoK

ORGANIZATION OF THE CMBOK

'Knowledge Areas' and 'Knowledge Components'

For the purposes of the CMBoK, 'knowledge' relating to effective Change Management is organized into thirteen *Knowledge Areas*. Each Knowledge Area describes a major aspect of the underpinning knowledge and practical experience expected of an effective Change Manager.

Within each Knowledge Area there are three or more *Knowledge Components* – distinct but related subsets of the Knowledge Area under which they are described.

TOOLS AND TEMPLATES

Where to find help with practical tools and templates

Tools and templates are an important resource for Change Managers; their knowledge helps them to decide which specific tools or templates to use when. The Change Management Institute is an independent professional body and therefore does not endorse any specific toolsets or methodologies. However, in support of our members we have collected a number of generic tools, templates and models, which are available on our website at: www.change-management-institute.com/tools-models.

COMMON TERMS USED IN THE CMBOK

Organizations describe their change plans in different ways

Organizations use a wide variety of terms when describing the plans associated with change processes. This is influenced by their approach to project, programme and portfolio management. For consistency we have adopted the following terminology throughout the CMBoK:

Change initiative: except where the context requires an alternative, we have used this term as a general expression to include any intentional change process, including those constituted formally as a change portfolio, change programme or change project.

Change management plan: we have used this term for a plan that typically includes change impact, the organization's change readiness, capability and capacity for change, meeting key learning needs and achievement of outcomes.

Benefits realization plan: we have used this term for a plan that typically identifies the benefit owners, includes a summary of the benefits of a change initiative, states the timing of their expected realization and schedules benefit reviews.

The Change Management Institute

Delivery plan: our use of this term applies to a plan that can be created at various levels of a change initiative (programme or project) and typically includes the timing and sequence of key implementation tasks, delivery of outputs and transition to the business.

GENERAL REFERENCES

The references used throughout this edition are those that practitioners have often cited as being of significant value. A number of these cover several of the areas of knowledge in the CMBoK and are listed below for ease of access.

Cameron, E. and Green, M., 2012. *Making Sense of Change Management: a complete guide to the models, tools and techniques of organizational change.* 3rd ed. London: Kogan Page.

Huczynski, A.A. and Buchanan, D.A., 2007. *Organizational Behaviour.* 6th ed. Harlow: Pearson Education.

Kotter, J.P., 2012. *Leading Change.* 2nd ed. Boston, MA: Harvard Business Review Press.

Reference should also be made to related CMI publications:

CMI, 2012. *Organisational Change Management Maturity.* [pdf]

CMI, 2012. *Change Management Practitioner Competencies v.2.2.* [pdf]

Both are available at:

www.change-management-institute.com/tools-models

Editorial note on spellings

During the review process we received strong feedback about our use of 'z' in spelling words (such as 'organization'). Several reviewers expressed the opinion that these words should be spelt with 's'. Although the 's' spelling of organization and similar words is common in the UK and Australia, both 's' and 'z' spellings are acceptable in British English. In fact, the Oxford English Dictionary uses the 'z' spelling for its own 'house style'. We have adopted the same convention.

PRINCE2® is a registered trade mark of AXELOS Limited
MSP® is a registered trade mark of AXELOS Limited
M_o_R® is a registered trade mark of AXELOS Limited
P3M3® is a registered trade mark of AXELOS Limited
MoP® is a registered trade mark of AXELOS Limited
MoV® is a registered trade mark of AXELOS Limited
PMBOK® is a registered trade mark of Project Management Institute Inc.
Prosci® is a registered trade mark of Prosci Inc.
The Myers-Briggs Type Indicator® and MBTI® are registered trade marks of the MBTI Trust Inc.

Contents

You don't have to read the CMBoK from front to back – all the Knowledge Areas can be read separately. Use the navigation trees throughout the CMBoK to find your way to the topics of most interest to you.

The Change Management Institute

Knowledge Area 1: A Change Management Perspective

The overarching theories behind change

BACKGROUND

A thorough knowledge of change principles and how to apply them is a key reason that change managers exist as a distinct professional group. They do not work in isolation, but connect intentionally and systematically with professionals in a range of disciplines to enable effective change to take place. However, the wide understanding that effective change managers have of different perspectives on change enables them to contribute to the organization's success by:

- Advocating appropriate and effective change management practices;

- Defining change, placing it in context;

- Engaging people to the extent necessary for the change initiative to succeed;

- Helping manage the benefits of a change to both the unit and the wider organization;

- Supporting development and execution of comprehensive plans for change initiatives;

- Facilitating the change process for individuals, teams and the wider organization;

- Ensuring that change becomes embedded in the organization – the new 'business as usual'; and

- Advising and coaching senior colleagues who are sponsoring or leading change initiatives.

Change managers are aware of research findings since the 1990s showing the high proportion of change initiatives that fail to deliver the promised benefits. They use this to highlight the importance of a relentless focus on good change management practices, which have been shown to increase the probability of successful change by a factor of four. They understand how to structure a change initiative, and how to work with operational managers to ensure that it has the best possible chance of delivering the expected benefits.

Turning from benefits to costs, the direct costs of a change initiative are often relatively easy to identify. It is, however, also easy for change sponsors to 'miss' some major categories of cost which will prove critical to successful change implementation. Change managers understand research on the factors that impact the success rates of change initiatives. They use this information to influence colleagues, ensuring that *realistic* assessments are made of the costs of implementing change.

Effective change managers are able to apply to their organization a range of research (theories and models) about change at all levels – from the strategic to the human-scale of individuals and small groups. This applied understanding leads to greater engagement of everyone involved in the change process. Change managers also understand the procedural and structural 'levers' an organization can use to facilitate change. They understand how to apply these to organizations to drive and sustain the required outcomes.

Because change managers understand the overarching theories behind change, they can help protect organizations from beginning or continuing with flawed initiatives. They support organizations in applying the best available practice in managing the change process. They also greatly improve the realization of the benefits of change, helping organizations to deliver full value from the initiatives they do undertake.

KNOWLEDGE COMPONENTS

These Knowledge Components are essential aspects of a change management perspective:

1. Why change management matters

2. Change and the individual

3. Change and the organization

4. Key roles in organizational change

5. Organizational culture and change

6. Emergent change

CHANGE MANAGEMENT IN PRACTICE

Effective change managers have a broad understanding of organizational change that helps an organization's leaders and managers work through change. This awareness is maintained by following developments in change management thinking (concepts and theories), research and best practice. Change managers often spend time with people to explain how change can be successfully managed through adoption of different models of and approaches to change. This also involves them in working closely with Organization Development (OD) and Human Resources (HR) professionals, to ensure that people involved in or affected by change are understood, supported and motivated.

A key responsibility of change managers is to help senior managers select suitable approaches from a range of change models. They ensure the right people are involved in the right change 'steps' and know that building 'agility' throughout an organization (such as cross-boundary working) increases the culture and capacity for continuous renewal and change. Change managers also understand the distinctive contributions that different individuals and groups make to successful change. They act as 'agents' for change and work with individuals and groups, at different levels, to help them make appropriate contributions.

Effective change managers recognize the nature and effect of 'cultural sensitivities' on change in an organization. This enables them to help leaders and managers develop appropriate strategies for developing the culture, promoting change and addressing resistance.

Effective change managers understand that not all change can be scheduled and planned and help senior managers in an organization recognize the features of complex 'emergent change'. They help create a supportive environment for leading and effecting such change.

**HOW THIS KNOWLEDGE AREA SUPPORTS
THE CMI CHANGE MANAGEMENT PRACTITIONER COMPETENCIES**

Related Change Manager Practitioner Competencies	1.1 Why change matters	1.2 Change and the individual	1.3 Change and the organization	1.4 Key roles in organizational change	1.5 Organizational culture and change	1.6 Emergent change
Facilitating Change	O	O	O		O	O
Strategic Thinking	O		O		O	O
Thinking & Judgement		O	O			
Influencing Others	O	O	O	O	O	
Coaching for Change	O	O	O	O	O	O
Project Management	O				O	
Communication Skills	O	O	O			
Self Management		O				

KEY REFERENCES FOR THIS KNOWLEDGE AREA

Cameron, E. and Green, M., 2012. *Making Sense of Change Management: a complete guide to the models, tools and techniques of organizational change.* 3rd ed. London: Kogan Page.

Dunphy, D.C. and Griffiths, A., 1994. *Theories of Organisational Change as Models of Intervention.* Sydney: Centre for Corporate Change (Australian Graduate School of Management at University of New South Wales).

Gilgeous, V., 1997. *Operations and the Management of Change.* Harlow, Essex: Pitman.

Huczynski, A.A. and Buchanan, D.A., 2007. *Organizational Behaviour.* 6th ed. Harlow: Pearson Education.

Kotter, J.P., 2012. *Leading Change.* 2nd ed. Boston, MA: Harvard Business Review Press.

Prosci, 2012. *Best Practices in Change Management,* Loveland, CO: Prosci.

Knowledge Component 1.1: Why change management matters

Change success rates and how to improve them

'It is not the strongest of the species that survives, nor the most intelligent that survives. It is the one that is the most adaptable to change.'

Charles Darwin

DEFINITION

The knowledge required to offer clear, concise and well-evidenced information about the role of effective change management in enabling successful change in organizations.

EXPLANATION

Knowledge in this area is necessary because effective change managers must be able to advocate the importance of good practice. They also need to articulate clearly the high-level factors that lead to effective change implementation.

When organization leaders or managers seek to initiate change, they are often optimistic about the process. They can see clearly how beneficial the proposed change will be, and assume others will see it just as easily. They have confidence that the skill they and their team have developed in (relatively) steady-state situations will transfer easily to change implementation. Often they define too narrowly the range of people who are likely to be affected. The change manager's ability to offer caution, based on good research, can help to define change more realistically.

However, it is not sufficient for change managers to disrupt unwarranted optimism. They must be able to explain in a few sentences – the 'elevator pitch' – what research shows about how to achieve successful change. This forms the basis of change managers' confidence that they can help their line colleagues to achieve a successful outcome.

KNOWLEDGE

The knowledge expected of an effective Change Manager is:

1. Current information about the success rates of change across a range of organizations. For two decades it appears this has been stuck at around 30% of change initiatives that are mostly or wholly successful although this figure is difficult to verify (Hughes, 2011).

2. The factors that have been shown to impact positively on the probability of change delivering the intended outcomes for the organization, and evidence of how effective change management practices support these factors (Prosci, 2012; PricewaterhouseCoopers, 2004; and LaClair and Rao, 2002).

See also:

Knowledge Component 4.3: Managing relationships and mobilizing stakeholders

Knowledge Area 7: Change Readiness, Planning and Measurement

3. The critical importance of preparing the organization and its people for change, and of the research that supports this.

4. The key considerations in designing the change process (such as Balogun and Hope–Hailey, 2008).

REFERENCES

APMG-International, 2013. *Change Management Practitioner Handbook*. Version 1.5. High Wycombe, Buckinghamshire: APMG-International. Section 3.

Balogun, J. and Hope-Hailey, V., 2008. *Exploring Strategic Change*. 3rd ed. Harlow: Pearson Education.

Change Track Insight, 2008. *On The Path to High Performance: Three fundamentals of successful change*. Sydney, Australia: Change Track Research.

Changefirst, 2010. *The ROI for Change Management*. Haywards Heath, UK: Changefirst.

Ferris, K., 2013. *ITSM Solution Projects Need Organisational Change Management*. Australia: Macanta Consulting.

Hiatt, J.M. and Creasey, T.J., 2012. *Change Management: The people side of change*. 2nd ed. Loveland, Colorado, USA: Prosci Research.

Hughes, M., 2011. *Do 70 Per Cent of All Organizational Change Initiatives Really Fail?* Journal of Change Management, December 2011, 11(4), pp.451–464.

IBM., 2008. *Making Change Work*. New York: IBM.

LaClair, J.A. and Rao, R.P., 2002. *Helping Employees Embrace Change*, McKinsey Quarterly. November 2002.

Moorhouse Consulting, 2013. *Barometer On Change 2013: If a change is worth doing, focus on doing it well*. London: Moorhouse.

PricewaterhouseCoopers, 2004. *Boosting Business Performance through Programme and Project Management*. [pdf], available at: http://www.pwc.com/us/en/operations-management/assets/pwc-global-project-management-survey-first-survey-2004.pdf [Accessed 24 September 2013]

Prosci, 2012. *Best Practices in Change Management*, Loveland, CO: Prosci.

Knowledge Component 1.2:
Change and the individual

Major models of the individual change process

'All changes, even the most longed for, have their melancholy; for what we leave behind us is a part of ourselves; we must die to one life before we can enter another.'

Anatole France

DEFINITION

Knowledge of key insights from the fields of psychology and sociology about how individuals (and groups or teams of individuals) experience change and how these insights can be used to support people through change processes.

EXPLANATION

Social science research over more than fifty years provides information about how people respond to change. One of the distinctive contributions effective change managers make to their organization is their understanding of the human side of change. It is their role to ensure that these research insights are applied effectively to the organization's change initiatives.

Models of individual and group change see change as a function of time – people go through a process. The many individuals affected will each experience the change in their own unique ways, and each of these may be different from the change process as seen from an organizational perspective. In many cases effective change managers have an educational role. They must help managers and leaders at all levels to focus on doing the things that engage, support or challenge people appropriately. They may also provide help for individuals facing change.

Source: Kublar-Ross (1969)

In applying their expertise in this area, change managers may have the support of Organization Development (OD) or Human Resources (HR) professionals. Effective change managers make full use of this professional expertise from supportive colleagues. However it is the Change Manager's task to ensure that those who are sponsoring or leading change recognize and understand the people-side of a change initiative, and that those who are charged with designing and implementing it manage it effectively.

One key aspect of individual change is the learning process. Learning theory helps change managers to understand the steps that they can take to improve the rate and effectiveness of learning. It allows them to factor into their plans the impact on performance of people learning new knowledge, skills and behaviour patterns.

See also:

Knowledge Component 5.1: Theory of effective communicating

Knowledge Component 7.1: Building individual motivation to change

Knowledge Component 7.3: Planning for resistance

Knowledge Area 9: Education and Learning Support

KNOWLEDGE

The knowledge expected of an effective Change Manager is:

1. A range of perspectives on human motivation, including:

    *   The use and limitations of rewards and sanctions as sources of motivation to change;
    *   The individual drives that shape behaviour, and their role in helping or hindering change; and
    *   Expectancy theories of motivation (see Huczynski and Buchanan, 2007, pp.251–254).

2. One or more models of individual difference that enable the Change Manager to tailor messages to meet the needs of different people, and to engage people with different personal styles. Common examples include Learning Styles and the Myers-Briggs Type Indicator® (MBTI®).

3. The core psychological conditions needed to enable individuals to change, grow and develop (Rogers, 1967).

4. The difference between 'planned change' and 'human transition', and the implications of this for change initiatives. The effective Change Manager is able to describe appropriate leadership for people at different stages of this process (Bridges, 2009).

5. The Transition curve (also called 'change curve' or 'coping cycle') and its contribution to understanding the human response to change, including:

    *   The ability to identify the main behaviour patterns associated with different stages of the curve; and
    *   An understanding of appropriate and inappropriate responses from supervisors and leaders to those behaviour patterns (Adams, Hayes and Hopson, 1976).

6. Typical ways in which individuals express their resistance to change, how to identify these and how to respond appropriately (Block, 2000).

REFERENCES

Adams, J., Hayes, J. and Hopson, B., 1976. *Transition: understanding and managing personal change.* London: Martin Robertson.

Block, P., 2000. *Flawless Consulting: a guide to getting your expertise used.* 2nd ed. San Francisco, CA: Jossey-Bass Pfeiffer.

Bridges, W., 2009. *Managing Transitions: making the most of change.* 3rd ed. London: Nicholas Brealey.

Briggs Myers, I. and Myers, P.B., 1995. *Gifts Differing: understanding personality type.* 2nd ed. Mountain View, CA: CPP Inc.

Cameron, E. and Green, M., 2012. *Making Sense of Change Management: a complete guide to the models, tools and techniques of organizational change.* 3rd ed. London: Kogan Page. Chapter 1 and pp.134–138, pp.190–192.

Honey, P. and Mumford, A., 1982. *Manual of Learning Styles.* Oxford, Oxfordshire: Peter Honey Publications.

Huczynski, A.A. and Buchanan, D.A., 2007. *Organizational Behaviour.* 6th ed. Harlow, Essex: Pearson Education. Chapters 4, 5, 8 and 18.

Kübler-Ross, E., 1969. *On Death and Dying.* Toronto: Macmillan.

Rogers, C.R., 1967. *On Becoming A Person: a therapist's view of psychotherapy.* London: Constable.

Knowledge Component 1.3:
Change and the organization

Major models of the organizational change process

'No great improvements in the lot of mankind are possible, until a great change takes place in the fundamental constitution of their modes of thought.'

John Stuart Mill

DEFINITION

Knowledge of key insights about organizational change and how it can be made effective, drawn from a range of approaches.

EXPLANATION

To be effective in their role, change managers need to understand how organizational change works – and why it often does not. This goes beyond the need to explain the value of change management and addresses the way change actually works in the organization.

Observations of, and research into, this area have long roots. Effective change managers distinguish the scope and scale of change and calibrate the change approach accordingly. They understand Kurt Lewin's classic 'unfreeze–change–refreeze' model and ensure that the right actions are in place at each phase to achieve lasting change. They can apply one of the 'n-step' approaches to change, such as John Kotter's '8-step process for leading change' (Kotter, 1995), ensuring that the right people are involved, and that they attend properly to each step. They are also familiar with approaches based on systems theory. They can nurture small scale initiatives, growing and shaping them into wider, more effective and more far-reaching initiatives.

Finally effective change managers understand that some organization structures and cultures tend to restrict change, while others enable it. They know how to help build an agile organization, where change is embedded in the design of the organization as a continuous process of renewal (Kotter 2012b).

KNOWLEDGE

The knowledge expected of an effective Change Manager is:

1. How change initiatives vary, and require different approaches. Local and narrowly-defined changes need effective change management, as do corporate transformations; however, the strategy for the change and the effort applied must be tailored to the circumstances.

2. The different beliefs about organizations that leaders might hold based on engineering, sociological, ecological or other metaphors. How these may be used to inform thinking about a variety of change processes from simple IT systems implementations to fundamental cultural transformation (Morgan, 2006).

3. Organization culture, and its ability to support or inhibit the change process.

4. The way that Lewin's 'unfreeze–change–refreeze' model can be applied to a change process and the actions that managers, leaders and change agents need to take at each stage to facilitate effective change.

5. One or more of the prescriptions for organizational change (so-called 'n-step' models) including the key people and roles at each stage, and the main business to be concluded at that stage.

6. How application of 'systems thinking' can help develop and embed sustainable change initiatives. This includes understanding the role of feedback systems and the concept of the 'learning organization'.

7. How the boundaries inherent in traditional hierarchical organization structures can inhibit change. How alternative and parallel structures can be used to enable change to happen more freely.

See also:

Knowledge Component 2.1: Aligning change with strategy

Knowledge Component 2.2: Drivers of change

Knowledge Component 7.2: Building organizational readiness to change

Knowledge Component 11.5 Embedding change

REFERENCES

Cameron, E. and Green, M., 2012. *Making Sense of Change Management: a complete guide to the models, tools and techniques of organizational change.* 3rd ed. London: Kogan Page. Chapter 3.

Dunphy, D. and Stace, D., 1994. *Translating Business Strategy into Action: transitions, transformations and turnarounds.* Sydney: McGraw-Hill.

Huczynski, A.A. and Buchanan, D.A., 2007. *Organizational Behaviour.* 6th ed. Harlow, Essex: Pearson Education. Chapter 18.

Kanter, R.M., 1983. *The Change Masters: corporate entrepreneurs at work.* London: George Allen & Unwin.

Kotter, J.P., 1995. Leading Change: why transformation efforts fail. *Harvard Business Review,* May–June.

Kotter, J.P., 2012a. *Leading Change.* 2nd ed. Boston, MA: Harvard Business Review Press.

Kotter, J.P., 2012b. Accelerate: how the most innovative companies capitalize on today's rapid-fire strategic challenges and still make their numbers. *Harvard Business Review,* November, 90(11), pp.44–58.

Lewin, K. (ed.), 1951. *Field Theory in Social Science: selected theoretical papers.* New York: Harper & Row.

Morgan, G., 2006. *Images of Organization.* 4th ed. London: Sage.

Senge, P.M., 1993. *The Fifth Discipline: the art and practice of the learning organization.* London: Century.

Senge, P. et al., 1999. *The Dance Of Change: the challenge of sustaining momentum in learning organizations.* London: Nicholas Brealey.

Stace, D. and Dunphy, D., 1991. Beyond Traditional Paternalistic and Developmental Approaches to Organizational Change and Human Resource Strategies. *The International Journal of Human Resources Management,* December, 2(3), pp.263–283.

Knowledge Component 1.4:
Key roles in organizational change

Sponsors, change agents and other key players

'There is nothing more difficult to take in hand, more perilous to conduct, or more uncertain in its success, than to take the lead in the introduction of a new order of things. The challenges of change are always hard. It is important that we begin to unpack those challenges that confront this nation and realize that we each have a role that requires us to change and become more responsible for shaping our own future.'

Niccolo Machiavelli, The Prince (1532)

DEFINITION

How the roles of individuals and groups associated with a change initiative may be defined and fulfilled in order to maximise the probability of the initiative's success.

EXPLANATION

NOTE: This section of the CMBoK is not about leadership as such. Leadership principles are addressed elsewhere (see sidebar). This section is about role clarity for all involved in successful change.

There can be many triggers for change in an organization. These include business performance, external threats, market opportunities, customer requirements and many others. However, all change initiatives start with an idea that leads to a proposal for change. The source of the idea might be an individual or (sometimes) a group of people.

To gain traction in an organization the idea must be picked up by someone with the authority and drive to make something happen – a sponsor. There is substantial research to suggest that having appropriate and effective sponsorship may be the single most significant determinant of the success of a change initiative.

Senior and middle management, supervisors and people at all levels who are impacted by the change need to be involved appropriately for the change to be implemented and embedded. Effective Change Managers:

- Understand the distinctive contributions that these different individuals and groups make to successful change;

- Are able to articulate and clarify the main expectations of each;

- Know how to act themselves as agents for change; and

- Coach, enable and support others who need to perform this function at various levels of the organization – sometimes without formal authority or recognition.

See also:

Knowledge Component 1.5: Organization culture and change

Knowledge Area 4: Stakeholder Strategy

Knowledge Component 7.2: Building organizational readiness to change

Knowledge Component 9.3: Behavioural change and coaching

Knowledge Component 12.1: Leadership principles

Knowledge Component 12.2: Building team effectiveness

KNOWLEDGE

The knowledge expected of an effective Change Manager is:

1. The key activities of leaders and contributors to change, who are:

   • Originators of proposals for change;
   • Senior sponsors of change;
   • Line managers and leaders at various levels;
   • People impacted by change; or
   • Others who support the change process (such as change agents).

2. The role of the sponsor in:

   • Maintaining a profile for the initiative and championing it in a consistent manner;
   • Obtaining the resources required;
   • Gaining the continuing commitment and involvement of senior and line management;
   • Aligning the organization's infrastructure, environment and reward systems with the initiative; and
   • Ensuring alignment of the particular initiative with other organization initiatives and with its wider strategic goals.

3. The role of the change agent. This includes aspects of both the role of the change manager and the roles of others who may act as change agents in support of the change. Change managers need:

   • A well-developed concept of what the role of the change agent is (and what it is not);
   • A clear model of the process associated with change agency or consulting, especially of contracting with those in formal leadership positions;
   • A practical understanding of organizational culture and how it is maintained;
   • Insights into sources of power in organizations, and how to achieve influence without authority; and
   • An applied understanding of how to coach colleagues.

4. The ways in which middle management can be engaged and become effective advocates for change within their areas. The ways in which they can become barriers to, or distorters of, effective communication.

5. The ways in which the variety of team structures found in organizations can be made more effective and can be used to support change.

REFERENCES

Balogun, J. and Hailey, V.H., 2008. *Exploring Strategic Change.* 3rd ed. Harlow, Essex: Pearson Education.

Block, P., 2000. *Flawless Consulting: a guide to getting your expertise used.* 2nd ed. San Francisco, CA: Jossey-Bass Pfeiffer.

Cameron, E. and Green, M., 2012. *Making Sense of Change Management: a complete guide to the models, tools and techniques of organizational change.* 3rd ed. London: Kogan Page. Chapter 5 and pp.166–174.

Huczynski, A.A. and Buchanan, D.A., 2007. *Organizational Behaviour.* 6th ed. Harlow, Essex: Pearson Education. Chapter 18.

Kanter, R.M., 1983. *The Change Masters: corporate entrepreneurs at work.* London: George Allen & Unwin.

O'Neill, M., 2007. *Executive Coaching with Backbone and Heart.* 2nd ed. San Francisco, CA: Jossey-Bass.

Prosci, 2012. *Best Practices in Change Management,* Loveland, CO: Prosci. pp.59–70.

Schein, E.H., 1985. *Organizational Culture and Leadership.* San Francisco, CA: Jossey-Bass.

Senge, P. et al., 1999. *The Dance Of Change: the challenge of sustaining momentum in learning organizations.* London: Nicholas Brealey.

Knowledge Component 1.5:
Organizational culture and change

How cultural factors affect the change process

'In today's business environment, significant transformation cannot happen without the simultaneous transformation of a critical mass of leaders' and employees' mindsets and behaviour. Conscious transformation means attending to the consciousness of the people in your organization, including your own.'

Beyond Change Management
Dean Anderson and Linda Ackerman Anderson

DEFINITION

Organizational culture is the unspoken, often unrecognized, system of beliefs and expectations that structures the way in which the people in the organization view what is appropriate, or even possible behaviour. Although more deeply-embedded than this suggests, culture has been described as 'the way we do things around here'.

EXPLANATION

Organizational culture does not arise by accident. It is the accumulation of (perfectly valid) organizational experience and belief about 'what works'. This creates a value system that can be strong. However, this deeply-embedded system of values and beliefs, established under one set of (necessarily past) circumstances, frequently comes into conflict with the requirements of the organization to adapt for the future.

Organizational agility (itself a cultural characteristic) results from careful attention to helping people to regard change as a positive and valuable thing. Inattention to developing such agility means that even simple, mechanistic changes of procedure can meet resistance that has its roots in a cultural lack of agility.

More complex changes are likely to include elements that touch not only on beliefs about change itself, but which conflict with particular beliefs in the organization about the way things 'should' be or the way they 'should not' be done, creating additional resistance. Effective change managers identify the cultural sensitivities that a particular change impacts on. They develop strategies for promoting change in both the specific cultural 'artefact' that is creating resistance and in the culture of the organization with regard to change more generally.

An awareness of culture, the insight to recognize its contribution to change readiness and resistance, and the understanding of strategies leaders can use to shape culture are all part of the personal toolkit of effective change managers.

KNOWLEDGE

The knowledge expected of an effective Change Manager is:

1. A clear definition of 'culture' in an organizational context.

2. A useful mental model that describes some of the key dimensions of culture (such as Hofstede, 2010; Trompenaars and Hampden-Turner, 2012).

3. The impact of organizational culture on different types of change and on the ease with which each can be implemented.

4. The role of organizational leadership in establishing, maintaining and changing culture, including the cultural 'levers' available to senior leaders.

REFERENCES

Hofstede, G., Hofstede, G.J. and Minkov M., 2010. *Cultures and Organizations: software of the mind.* 3rd ed. New York: McGraw Hill.

Schein, E.H., 1985. *Organizational Culture and Leadership.* San Francisco, CA: Jossey-Bass.

Taylor, C., 2005. *Walking the Talk: building a culture for success.* London: Random House.

Trompenaars, F. and Hampden-Turner, C., 2012. *Riding the Waves of Culture: understanding diversity in global business.* 3rd ed. London: Nicholas Brealey.

See also:

Knowledge Area 7.2: Building organizational readiness to change

Knowledge Component 7.3: Planning for resistance

Knowledge Component 1.6:
Emergent change

Change that cannot be scheduled

'One way to find food for thought is to use the fork in the road, the bifurcation that marks the place of emergence in which a new line of development begins to branch off.'

William Irwin Thompson, Philosopher

DEFINITION

Emergent change occurs when a need for changed patterns of values and behaviour in the organization is identified, when the direction of such change is specified, and when organization leaders take coordinated action to stimulate, encourage and reinforce these new patterns.

EXPLANATION

While effective change requires focused and intentional effort by senior leaders, not all change can be scheduled and planned. Where the core of the change is to systems, structures, processes and practices, then planning and scheduling is possible. However, where that core change is in the discretionary decisions people make about their patterns of values and behaviours, no dates can be fixed in advance. People will engage with new patterns of behaviour individually and in their own time.

This does not mean that change managers and organization leaders are helpless. Careful thought can be given to the direction of change that is required, and to the indicators which will show that progress is being made. Leaders can be intentional about their own words, challenging existing paradigms and supporting new ones. They can be sure that their own actions model consistently the new expected behaviours. They can celebrate and mark milestones on the journey and remain open to new data that may lead to redefinition of the direction. Changes in values and behaviour are seldom linear or predictable.

Effective change managers help their senior colleagues and organization leaders to:

- Set appropriate direction;

- Find relevant behavioural indicators;

- Identify tipping points; and

- Create an environment supportive of the new values and behaviour.

In these ways they are able to support these complex processes.

KNOWLEDGE

The knowledge expected of an effective Change Manager is:

1. Categories of change that are likely to contain components of 'emergent change' and how to define those components.

2. Ways to define and describe the patterns of behaviour and values that will characterize the organization when the change has been successful.

3. Leadership strategies to achieve change in a world that is 'volatile, uncertain, complex and ambiguous' (VUCA).

4. How the concepts of critical mass, 'nudge' and 'tipping point' can be used to maintain momentum towards the desired and defined future state.

REFERENCES

Burns, B., 2009. *Managing Change.* 5th ed. Harlow, Essex: Pearson Education.

Lawrence, K., 2013. *Developing Leaders in a VUCA Environment.* (UNC Kenan-Flagler Business School) [pdf] Available at: <http://www.kenan-flagler.unc.edu/~/media/Files/documents/executive-development/developing-leaders-in-a-vuca-environment.pdf> [Accessed 25 September 2013].

Schein, E.H., 1985. *Organizational Culture and Leadership.* San Francisco, CA: Jossey-Bass.

See also:

Knowledge Component 2.2: Drivers of change

Knowledge Component 2.3: Change definition

Knowledge Area 11.4: Achieving critical mass

Knowledge Area 2: Defining Change

What is the change?

BACKGROUND

Change in organizations can have wide-ranging implications. Change must be understood thoroughly for it to be successful. This requires early and effective stakeholder engagement to establish and achieve a common understanding of the reasons why change is needed. This will involve understanding the internal and external drivers for change and where it fits in the bigger picture. Clarifying the purpose, scope, boundaries and business impacts of the change will increase the likelihood of a successful outcome. Another key element is to understand the capability and capacity of the organization to effect the change. Finally, to know whether change has been a success, the benefits from the change must be clear. Where 'emergent change' is evident in an organization, often reflecting long-term change factors and complexity, the specific drivers and required responses (and outcomes) may not always be easy to define.

Stakeholders will view change from many different perspectives. Effective change managers help an organization to carry out a detailed diagnosis and analysis of needs, issues, the environment and priorities for change. They also work closely with other roles – such as business and requirements analysts and subject matter experts – to define and design the changes. The resulting change management plan and supporting business case must be aligned to the organization's corporate strategic goals. It should also match the needs and expectations of stakeholders at all levels within the organization. Effective change managers know that everyone involved must use a clear and concise definition of the change in a consistent manner (where this is feasible – see above on 'emergent change') to maintain focus and guide priorities. It also ensures that the change initiative is focused on the desired outcomes and benefits, including ongoing tracking and realization of benefits beyond the change. All of this must be set out in the change management plan for the change initiative. At a detailed level, these requirements will be set out in the programme and project delivery plans.

KNOWLEDGE COMPONENTS

These Knowledge Components are essential to the successful definition of change:

1. Aligning change with strategy
2. Drivers of change
3. Change definition
4. Developing vision
5. Scenario design and testing

DEFINING 'CHANGE' IN PRACTICE

Effective change managers help ensure that a change initiative is fully and continually aligned to the organization's strategic goals and objectives. When change requirements are being scoped change managers work closely with change sponsors, project managers and specialists to help build a complete picture of change and how the organization will be affected. This enables a change strategy to be developed that reflects the respective forces and influences on the change. As part of a multi-disciplinary change team, effective change managers help facilitate the participation of key business area stakeholders in the creation and communication of a vision for change. They also provide input to the scoping and capture of specific change requirements and options, ensuring that different business scenarios are appropriately tested and approved. The Change Manager contributes to an assessment of the organization's capability and capacity to deliver the defined change successfully. This involves looking at the business and technical skills of its people and the resources (financial and otherwise) that are available.

HOW THIS KNOWLEDGE AREA SUPPORTS
THE CMI CHANGE MANAGEMENT PRACTITIONER COMPETENCIES

Related Change Manager Practitioner Competencies	2.1 Aligning change with strategy	2.2 Drivers for change	2.3 Change definition	2.4 Develop vision	2.5 Scenario design and testing
Facilitating Change	O			O	O
Strategic Thinking		O	O	O	O
Thinking & Judgement	O				
Influencing Others				O	
Coaching for Change	O				
Specialist Expertise – Learning & Development	O				O
Specialist Expertise – Communication	O				

KEY REFERENCES FOR THIS KNOWLEDGE AREA

Blake, I. and Bush, C., 2009. *Project Managing Change*. Harlow, Essex: Pearson Education.

Cabinet Office, 2011. *Managing Successful Programmes*. 4th ed. London: TSO.

Cabinet Office, 2011. *Management of Portfolios*. London: TSO.

Knowledge Component 2.1:
Aligning change with strategy

Understanding the organization's business direction

'You've got to eat while you dream. You've got to deliver on short-range commitments, while you develop a long-range strategy and vision and implement it. The success of doing both. Walking and chewing gum if you will. Getting it done in the short-range, and delivering a long-range plan, and executing on that.'

Jack Welch

DEFINITION

This is the alignment of the change initiative and its components with the strategic goals of the organization. It can also mean using a change initiative to drive the development and delivery of strategy. The process of alignment takes account of the organization's business environment and of business changes designed to meet the needs of that environment.

EXPLANATION

Effective change managers ensure that each change initiative aligns with the organization's strategic corporate goals. Maintaining focus on strategy during the full change process ensures clarity and consistency and increases the likelihood of achieving the outcomes and benefits envisaged. This sustained focus is usually achieved through creating a clear vision for change.

An organization's business environment is also subject to change, resulting in changes to corporate strategy that impact on ongoing or planned change initiatives. Ongoing alignment of change initiatives with strategy ensures that business changes are assessed and taken into account. This becomes more important as the size and complexity of the business grows and must be reflected in the development of the change management plan.

Effective change managers know that clarifying the organization's strategic goals and intentions is important but they are not expected to be strategic analysts. The task of aligning change with strategy involves:

- Clear identification and understanding of the organization's corporate strategic aims, objectives and performance targets;

- Linking change explicitly to achievement of the organization's strategic aims, objectives and performance targets, as well as to people's personal objectives, to aid behavioural change;

- Identifying and mapping the strategic links and dependencies between the organization's change initiatives – such as programmes and projects – to leverage new, and existing, change; and

- Raising awareness of the opportunities to integrate and optimize the outcomes and benefits of a change initiative, where it exists as part of an organization's wider strategic change portfolio.

See also:

Knowledge Area 3:
Managing Benefits

Knowledge Area 4:
Stakeholder Strategy

Knowledge Area 8:
Project Management

KNOWLEDGE

The knowledge expected of an effective Change Manager is:

1. Awareness of strategic analysis tools to help strategic decision-makers confirm, clarify and regularly review corporate strategic goals, objectives and targets.

2. Ways to use this information to define and direct, or redirect, the change initiative to increase the organization's flexibility and adaptability as needs and priorities change.

3. Methods of identifying, mapping and assessing the links and dependencies between an organization's change initiatives, programmes and projects, including incremental developments that may relate to longer-term 'emergent change'.

4. Awareness of good-practice approaches and methods in portfolio management prioritization and decision-making.

5. Forecasting, addressing and resolving organization-wide resource conflicts to achieve an acceptable balance between 'business as usual' and change tasks.

REFERENCES

Cabinet Office, 2011. *Managing Successful Programmes*. 4th ed. London: TSO.

Cabinet Office, 2011. *Management of Portfolios*. London: TSO.

The Knowledge Compass, 2006. *The Case for Strategic Alignment – White Paper.* [pdf] Available at: <http://www.knowledgecompanyinc.com/images/The_Case_for_Strategic_Alignment_-_vC010106.pdf> [Accessed 25 September 2013].

Knowledge Component 2.2:
Drivers of change

Understanding why change is needed

'I can't change the direction of the wind, but I can adjust my sails to always reach my destination.'

Jimmy Dean

DEFINITION

Identifying the drivers of change is the process of identifying the factors and major trends driving the need to change. It includes the use of these factors to maintain strategic focus and energy for the initiative during the change process. It provides the answers to the fundamental questions 'Why change?' and 'Why now?'

EXPLANATION

Change is a reflection of the ever-changing 'dynamics' of organizations. Organizations need to adapt flexibly to changing needs and priorities, whether externally or internally generated. Change drivers will include the need to respond to increased risk, a crisis or to exploit an opportunity. For change to be successful, the initial priority is to 'establish a sense of urgency'.

Effective change managers help the organization to raise awareness of the need for change and the impact this may have on the business, its people and customers. This understanding is reflected in the vision for change and provides an essential input to the development and delivery of the change management plan. Continual scanning and (re)assessment of the organization's business environment is an important ongoing activity.

Effective change managers understand that 'driving forces must outweigh resisting forces' (Lewin, 1951) for change to happen, through:

- Engaging with an organization's stakeholders to identify and map driving and resisting forces for change;

- Assessing the business environment in which the organization operates that has a direct impact on the change initiative;

- Scanning the organization's political, economic, social, technological, legal and environmental (PESTLE) position to test business assumptions and explore possible future state scenarios and trends;

Driving Forces

Restraining Forces

- Understanding the systemic nature of organizations, their formal and informal structures, processes, culture and communications; and

- Looking at the underlying causes of problems that change needs to address and mitigating risk.

See also:

Knowledge Area 3:
Managing Benefits

Knowledge Area 4:
Stakeholder Strategy

Knowledge Area 5:
Communication and
Engagement

Knowledge Area 6:
Change Impact

KNOWLEDGE

The knowledge expected of an effective Change Manager is:

1. Organizational culture, and the factors and influences that are specific to the organization's business sector or market.

2. Techniques for mapping, as well as environmental scanning, to identify and to analyse forces that are driving and resisting change, and addressing the emerging trends and issues (such as PESTLE and 'foresight' approaches).

3. Awareness of tools and techniques to capture and analyse an organization's internal and external influences (such as 'strengths, weaknesses, opportunities and threats' (SWOT).

4. Identifying the organization's systemic nature and applying 'systems thinking' concepts and techniques.

5. The use of this information to engage stakeholders and to create the change management plan.

REFERENCES

Barber, M., 2006. Wildcards: signals from a future near you. *Journal of Futures Studies,* 11(1), pp.75–94.

Cameron, E. and Green, M., 2012. *Making Sense of Change Management: a complete guide to the models, tools and techniques of organizational change.* 3rd ed. London: Kogan Page.

Checkland, P. and Scholes J., 1999. *Soft Systems Methodology in Action.* London: Wiley.

Conway, M., 2009. *Environmental Scanning: what it is and how to do it.* [pdf] Available at: <http://thinkingfutures.net/wp-content/uploads/2010/10/ES-Guide-April-09.pdf> [Accessed 25 September 2013].

Kotter, J.P., 2012. *Leading Change.* 2nd ed. Boston, MA: Harvard Business Review Press.

Lewin, K., 1951. *Field Theory in Social Science: selected theoretical papers.* New York: Harper and Row.

Morgan, G., 2006. *Images of Organization.* 4th ed. London: Sage.

Nadler, D.A. and Tushman, M.L., In: M.B. Nadler, ed., 1997. *Competing by Design: the power of organizational architecture.* New York, NY: Oxford Universal Press.

Senge, P. et al., 1999. *The Dance Of Change: the challenge of sustaining momentum in learning organizations.* London: Nicholas Brealey.

Knowledge Component 2.3:
Change definition

Agreeing what change is needed

'If you do not change direction, you may end up where you are heading.'
Lao Tzu

DEFINITION

Change definition is the process of developing clear and complete definitions of how the organization will be changed, the nature of the impact on stakeholders and business areas, and the specific changes which will be seen across the organization in behaviour, outputs and outcomes.

EXPLANATION

Not everyone in an organization will view change in the same way. There will be a wide mix of positive, negative and neutral responses to change. Nor will the path to change be smooth and problem-free. It is important to understand and communicate the 'big-picture' of change and help people to view change in its wider context. It will be equally important to draw out the key issues and concerns that people have about change. The objective is building and sharing an understanding of the change and how obstacles can be resolved.

Key questions will concern:

* *Who* the change affects (the stakeholders);

* *How* the effect will be felt (for example in terms of changed behaviours or responses);

* *What* the change will ultimately deliver (including intended outputs and outcomes); and

* *When* the change is needed or will happen (providing timelines and any rules or conditions that will apply).

As these aspects become clear, so will the understanding and commitment of stakeholders in achieving the change. This understanding lays the foundations for a more in-depth impact assessment.

Effective change managers know that defining change is both top-down (strategically driven) and bottom-up (responding to operational needs) reflecting variations in scale, complexity and difficulty. They actively support and facilitate their own and others' learning about change through:

* Understanding and critically examining the wider context and different perspectives and scenarios when scoping and defining change (also being aware of different perspectives on how organizations work);

- Creating a 'road-map' for change, which explores different stakeholder perspectives, change factors and features when responding to change drivers and influencing forces; and

- Systematically identifying, analysing and resolving obstacles to change, in order to arrive at informed conclusions and decisions. This includes comparing the current state ('as-is') and future state ('to-be') to identify gaps.

Effective change managers often work alongside experts in business and requirements analysis; however, they do not need to be experts in these fields themselves.

See also:

Knowledge Component 1.3: Change and the organization

Knowledge Component 4.1: Identifying and segmenting stakeholders

Knowledge Component 6.1: Assessing the impact of change

Knowledge Component 8.3: Change planning and scheduling

Knowledge Component 13.3: Process optimization in organizations

KNOWLEDGE

The knowledge expected of an effective Change Manager is:

1. Extracting and interpreting impact assessment information from business analysis and process mapping methods.

2. Identifying and exploring requirements for, and the characteristics of, change (the *why, who, what, when and how* of change).

3. Problem-solving techniques (including evaluative or weighted scoring methods) to discover and assess concerns and problem-areas as well as emerging themes and trends, and what caused them.

4. Awareness of approaches and techniques of analysis, options selection and decision-making support.

5. Availability and sources of appropriately skilled and experienced business and requirements analysts.

6. Selecting and applying a variety of organizational change models to explore different perspectives and approaches to change.

7. The content and information needed to create change management and delivery plans.

REFERENCES

Adzic, G., 2012. *Impact Mapping: making a big impact with software products and projects.* Woking: Provoking Thoughts Ltd.

Buzan, T., 1993. *The Mind Map Book: radiant thinking.* London: BBC Books.

Cabinet Office, 2011. *Management of Portfolios.* London: TSO.

Cabinet Office, 2011. *Managing Successful Programmes.* 4th ed. London: TSO.

Cameron, E. and Green, M., 2012. *Making Sense of Change Management: a complete guide to the models, tools and techniques of organizational change.* 3rd ed. London: Kogan Page.

De Bono, E., 1971. *Lateral Thinking for Management: a handbook.* London: Penguin Books.

Knowledge Component 2.4:
Developing vision

Focusing on the 'end-goal' for change

'Vision refers to a picture of the future with some implicit or explicit commentary on why people should strive to create that future.'

John P Kotter

DEFINITION

Developing vision is the collaborative process of creating a compelling vision of the 'end state' following successful completion of a change initiative, and developing an engaging narrative that connects the pre- and post-change states.

EXPLANATION

A clear vision for change enables an organization's leaders, managers and change sponsors to identify and communicate the desired end-goal, scope and boundaries of a change initiative. It enables the Change Manager, change team, stakeholders and the organization to understand the purpose of the change and to commit to the steps needed to make change work. A clear vision for change also helps people to focus on the wider organizational implications and opportunities. This includes identifying the impact change has on business strategy, plans and business activities and the need to adapt flexibly to the strategic change landscape.

Effective change managers make clear distinctions between an organization's strategic mission, goals, objectives and targets on the one hand and the creation of a vision and narrative for a change initiative on the other. This is achieved through:

* Early engagement with senior management and other key stakeholders to visualise the desired future state, including addressing the implications of 'no change';

* Creating a vision statement (expressed in various forms) that reflects a consensus view of change, together with the needs and priorities of the organization and its stakeholders relating to the change; and

* Creating a compelling 'story' for communicating the desired end-goal of change, motivating and inspiring stakeholders, and getting commitment at all levels of the organization.

See also:

Knowledge Area 4:
Stakeholder Strategy

Knowledge
Component 5.2:
Communicating
change

Knowledge
Component 5.3:
Communication
channels

Knowledge Area 10:
Facilitation

KNOWLEDGE

The knowledge expected of an effective Change Manager is:

1. Methods for facilitating stakeholder workshops to explore different viewpoints and perspectives.

2. Creative thinking methods and techniques to capture and explore ideas about the future state.

3. The structuring of methods to create, validate and secure buy-in and commitment to the stakeholders' vision statement.

4. Methods and approaches for communicating the vision to a variety of stakeholders using visionary and narrative or 'storytelling' approaches.

REFERENCES

Cabinet Office, 2011. *Managing Successful Programmes*. 4th ed. London: TSO.

Cameron, E. and Green, M., 2012. *Making Sense of Change Management: a complete guide to the models, tools and techniques of organizational change*. 3rd ed. London: Kogan Page.

Denning, S., 2005. *The Leader's Guide to Storytelling: mastering the art and discipline of business narrative*. San Francisco, CA: Wiley.

Kotter, J.P., 2012. *Leading Change*. 2nd ed. Boston, MA: Harvard Business Review Press.

Stevenson, D., 2008. *Story Theatre Method: strategic story telling in business*. 2nd ed. Colorado Springs, CO: Cornelia Press.

Knowledge Component 2.5:
Scenario design and testing

Exploring possible 'futures'

'Scenarios are stories. They consist of a setting, or situation state, one or more actors with personal motivations, knowledge, and capabilities, and various tools and objects that the actors encounter and manipulate. The scenario describes a sequence of actions and events that lead to an outcome'.

Rosson and Carroll

DEFINITION

Scenario design and testing is a process that ensures that the implications and requirements of a change initiative are properly explored and documented for a range of possible future scenarios.

EXPLANATION

The change vision and change impact assessment provide a picture of the change and its impact on the business and its stakeholders. The emerging change management plan lays the foundations for successful delivery. However, the proposed changes must first be appropriately tested and validated, as far as practicable. The purpose of testing is to ensure that the implications of change are thoroughly considered and the possible risks, opportunities and any negative effects are identified at an early stage. The greater the cost or complexity of change, the greater the importance of developing change scenarios that key stakeholders can test and validate. At a more detailed level this may include approaches such as 'operational readiness tests' and 'user acceptance tests'. Testing can include the use of pilots and simulations of different change scenarios. Scenario testing is an important input to the development, refinement and delivery of the change management plan and delivery plan, and to component parts of the change itself.

Effective change managers know that during a change initiative, scenario tests help to ensure:

- The high-level strategic vision is clearly connected to the local operational context (this helps stakeholders and stakeholder groups, at different levels in an organization, to understand the full implications of change); and

- Scenarios and tests are not theoretical or hypothetical, simplified or unrealistic and reflect 'real world' perspectives.

See also:

Knowledge Component 4.3: Managing relationships and mobilizing stakeholders

Knowledge Component 5.2: Communicating change

Knowledge Component 5.3: Communication channels

Knowledge Area 6: Change Impact

Knowledge Component 8.5: Transitioning to the business

Knowledge Component 13.3: Process optimization in organizations

KNOWLEDGE

The knowledge expected of an effective Change Manager is:

1. Methods, tools and techniques for:

   - Identifying and mapping future events, issues, trends and strategy (for example using the 'futures wheel' method for structured brainstorming to organise thinking about the future consequences of change);
   - Designing and testing realistic, appropriate and easy-to-evaluate change scenarios, including the use of pilots and simulations such as those used to test process flows and IT system functions;
   - Analysing gaps to highlight flaws and inherent problems, and to provide early warnings (for example regarding missing or ill-conceived requirements); and
   - Managing and interpreting information, including process mapping, data modelling, options analysis and optimizing the business case (costs, benefits and risks).

2. Awareness of 'systems thinking' methods and approaches to understand how different parts of the organization connect with each other.

3. Using a variety of approaches such as visualisation, story-boarding, simulation and other interactive or experiential techniques in addition to narrative/storytelling to achieve active participation of the different stakeholders.

REFERENCES

Glenn, J. C., Gordon, J. G., 2009. *Futures Research Methodology: The Millennium Project:* 3rd ed. [CD-ROM]. Available at: http://millennium-project.org/millennium/FRM-V3.html [Accessed 17 June 2013]

Kaner, C., 2003. *An Introduction to Scenario Testing.* [pdf] (Expanded version of text first published in the *Software Testing & Quality Engineering* (STQE) magazine.) Available at: <http://www.kaner.com/pdfs/ScenarioIntroVer4.pdf> [Accessed 17 June 2013].

Rosson, M.B. and Carroll, J.M., 2002. Scenario-based design. In: J. Jacko and A. Sears, eds., 2002. *The Human-Computer Interaction Handbook.* NJ: Lawrence Erlbaum Associates. pp.1032–1050.

Knowledge Area 3: Managing Benefits

Ensuring change delivers value

BACKGROUND

A benefit is defined as a 'measurable improvement' resulting from a change in the organization; and it offers an 'advantage to stakeholders', who are inside or outside the organization (Jenner, 2012). An example of a benefit is a saving in operating costs.

Changes can result in negative effects – sometimes called 'dis-benefits'. These effects are also addressed, as unintended consequences of change that will have a detrimental effect. An example of this is the loss of knowledge or experience when downsizing an organization. To be considered successful, a change initiative must have a clear definition of what success means and how this will be quantified. Benefits management is concerned with identifying, mapping, analysing, quantifying and realizing the benefits of a change initiative. It also focuses on alignment of benefits with the strategic goals of the organization.

Early identification of benefits helps to build commitment from (and plan engagement with) stakeholders. Benefits are a key input into the high-level vision statement, the detailed designs for change and the emerging, or evolving, business case. In some circumstances alignment of benefits might be necessary to satisfy or validate the rationale and justification for an enforced or imposed change. Benefits realization involves tracking and measuring the benefits, the negative effects and the achievement of desired outcomes.

The respective roles of the Change Manager and those of Programme or Project Managers are important for effective benefits management and realization. Change managers work with the business (often with business analysts, consultants and specialists in benefit management and realization) to help to identify, quantify and track the benefits from change. Programme and project managers ensure that projects deliver 'fit-for-purpose' products, on which benefits are dependent. In some organizations the role of benefits realization manager may be additionally defined, offering a specialized resource in this area.

Ultimate responsibility for benefits realization lies with business leaders and managers and effective change managers work closely with them to improve the chances of achieving the required outcomes.

KNOWLEDGE COMPONENTS

These Knowledge Components are essential to the successful management of benefits:

- Benefits management principles and processes

- Benefits identification, mapping and analysis

- Planning benefits realization

- Supporting benefits realization

MANAGING BENEFITS IN PRACTICE

The effective Change Manager works closely with key business stakeholders, project managers and specialists, helping to identify and quantify the benefits from a change initiative. It is important to ensure that benefits are aligned with the strategic aims of the organization, and to help business managers and staff to identify any possible negative effects of change. Change managers liaise with business and operational areas throughout the change process to ensure a continued focus on benefits. This includes ensuring that benefits are 'owned' by the appropriate business managers who also accept their accountability for benefits realization. Effective change managers act as a 'bridge' between the change initiative and the business areas impacted by change. They provide input to the development of benefit realization plans and support the business in capturing relevant measurement data for tracking benefit achievement.

HOW THIS KNOWLEDGE AREA SUPPORTS

THE CMI CHANGE MANAGEMENT PRACTITIONER COMPETENCIES

Related Change Manager Practitioner Competencies	3.1 Benefits management principles and processes	3.2 Benefits identification, mapping and analysis	3.3 Planning benefits realization	3.4 Supporting benefits realization
Facilitating Change	O	O	O	O
Strategic Thinking	O	O	O	O
Thinking & Judgement	O	O	O	O
Project Management	O		O	

KEY REFERENCES FOR THIS KNOWLEDGE AREA

Bradley, G., 2010. *Benefit Realisation Management: a practical guide to achieving benefits through change.* 2nd ed. Farnham, Surrey: Gower Publishing.

Jenner, S., 2012. *Managing Benefits: optimizing the return from investments.* London: APMG-International, TSO.

Knowledge Component 3.1:
Benefits management principles and processes

Ensuring a continued focus on benefits from change

'Effective benefits management is founded on a series of enabling factors or principles that represent the foundations upon which successful benefits management practices are built.'

Steve Jenner

DEFINITION

Benefits management is the process that identifies, maps, analyses, quantifies and ensures realization of the benefits of a change initiative. A set of established principles and practices (upon which effective benefits management is undertaken) underpins benefits management.

EXPLANATION

Benefits from change must contribute to at least one organizational or strategic objective. Benefits management seeks to optimize benefits – rather than to maximise them – and to diminish the impact of any negative effects of change. It also informs investment decisions at an organization's portfolio, programme and project levels. Defining an appropriate benefits management strategy and approach is essential to the success of a change initiative. It is also a key factor in quality management and review across the whole of a change initiative, to ensure continued focus on realization of benefits.

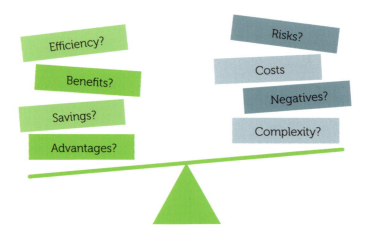

Effective change managers know that it is crucial for a change initiative to adopt consistent benefit management processes and practices. They work with programme or project managers as well as key business managers, contributing to the definition of the change initiative's benefits management strategy and approach. Effective change managers also make an active contribution to identifying, analysing, quantifying, planning, realizing and reviewing the benefits of a change initiative. The supporting processes and practices are integrated with the organization's strategic planning, portfolio, programme and project management approaches and its performance management systems.

KNOWLEDGE

The knowledge expected of an effective Change Manager is:

1. Principles and practices of benefits management and realization.

2. Awareness of change delivery methods that deliver sustained business value.

3. Performance and human resources management systems and how they may be affected by the new skills, behaviours and expected performance (i.e. the benefits) resulting from the change.

4. Governance frameworks to ensure accountability and responsibility for enabling business changes upon which benefits are dependent.

REFERENCES

Bradley, G., 2010. *Benefit Realisation Management: a practical guide to achieving benefits through change*. 2nd ed. Farnham, Surrey: Gower Publishing.

Cabinet Office, 2011. *Managing Successful Programmes*. 4th ed. London: TSO.

Jenner, S., 2012. *Managing Benefits: optimizing the return from investments*. London: APMG-International, TSO.

See also:

Knowledge Component 2.1: Aligning change with strategy

Knowledge Component 2.3: Change definition

Knowledge Area 6: Change impact

Knowledge Area 8: Project Management

Knowledge Component 13.1: The Change Manager and Human Resources

Knowledge Component 3.2:
Benefits identification, mapping and analysis

Ensuring a continued focus on benefits from change

'People can't always articulate what they want or need...You can't expect them to just give you the answers.'

Mark Pearson, Entrepreneur

DEFINITION

Benefits identification, mapping and analysis are iterative processes, using a variety of tools and techniques for articulating benefits and any negative effects of change. Likely benefits emerge from the change vision, the designs for change (including the definition of the 'to be' or future-state requirements), the business case, candidate projects and achievement of corporate objectives.

EXPLANATION

When defining requirements for change, benefits are articulated implicitly (for example through the vision statement) for the desired change. An explicit and full definition of benefits usually occurs when the full designs for change (including the definition of the 'to be' or future-state requirements) are created and the business case is finalised. Benefits include both tangible (such as cash savings) and intangible (such as enhanced image) types. Early identification of benefits can occur when mapping and exploring the business and process flows and interactions in an organization.

Effective change managers have an important role to play, working alongside programme and project managers, key business area managers, stakeholders, requirements analysts and specialists in benefits analysis. They know that early identification of benefits (together with any identified negative effects) of the change initiative is vital to success. A key factor is confirmation that all relevant and appropriate benefits and negative effects have been identified, and that relevant data has been captured and prioritized. This helps to ensure that the most significant benefits (those most clearly aligned to the primary investment objectives) are strongly supported and properly tracked. In turn, this lays the foundations for the specification and development of required business changes.

KNOWLEDGE

The knowledge expected of an effective Change Manager is:

1. Methods and techniques for 'benefit identification', mapping and analysis, including process and value-stream analysis techniques.

2. The typical pitfalls when quantifying benefits (such as double-counting, 'pseudo-financial' values and 'forcible extraction').

3. Managing content (for example by using 'benefit profiles') to capture and clarify relevant data and to establish benefit realization timescales, ownership and responsibility.

4. The relevance of benefits – and their negative effects – to creation and optimization of the business case for a change initiative.

See also:

Knowledge Component 2.3: Change definition

Knowledge Component 2.4: Developing vision

Knowledge Component 13.3: Process optimization in organizations

REFERENCES

Bradley, G., 2010. *Benefit Realisation Management: a practical guide to achieving benefits through change.* 2nd ed. Farnham, Surrey: Gower Publishing.

Cabinet Office, 2011. *Managing Successful Programmes.* 4th ed. London: TSO.

Jenner, S., 2012. *Managing Benefits: optimizing the return from investments.* London: APMG-International, TSO.

Kaplan, R.S., and Norton, D.P., 2004. *Strategy maps: converting intangible assets into tangible outcomes.* Boston, MA: Harvard Business School Press.

Knowledge Component 3.3:
Planning benefits realization

Working out the timetable for the expected returns

'In preparing for battle I have always found that plans are useless but planning is indispensable.'

Dwight D Eisenhower

DEFINITION

Planning benefits realization focuses on ensuring there is a process for planning, scheduling and reviewing the benefits of a change initiative and that the planned returns on the investment are achieved in accordance with the forecasts.

EXPLANATION

The results of benefits identification, mapping and analysis form the basis for planning benefits realization. The ultimate measure of the success of a change initiative is the 'measurable improvement' (the benefit or value) that is achieved. This, together with the achieved contribution towards the organization's objectives, provides the foundation – and driving force – for the change initiative. The benefits realization plan provides the timetable for benefits realization and the schedule of planned returns from the investment in change. It further provides the baseline against which portfolios, programmes and projects measure, track and control (review and report) benefits realization.

Effective change managers work alongside and collaborate closely with programme and project managers, key business area managers, stakeholders requirements analysts and specialists in benefits management. They know that business area managers must validate the benefits, and accept them as realistic and achievable. Clear accountability for benefits realization by business area managers is, therefore, essential.

The potential risks to achievement or optimization of benefits must also be assessed and managed. This includes assessing the organization's and the stakeholders' change readiness. Effective change managers also know the importance of verifying that the change initiative has changed the organization in identifiable and sustainable ways. This is a critical measure of ultimate success.

KNOWLEDGE

The knowledge expected of an effective Change Manager is:

1. Awareness of correct approaches, techniques and mechanisms for:

   - Financial analysis and prioritization;
   - Validation and prioritization of benefits (and negative effects of change); and
   - Baselining and measurement of benefits.

2. Factors in, and the criteria for, planning 'benefits realization' (taking into account the change readiness of the business area(s) and the stakeholders affected), and identifying risks to achievement of benefits.

3. Managing content (for example using a benefits realization plan along with ongoing tracking and reviews).

4. The roles of portfolio, programme and project managers during specific change initiatives for benefits management and for realization.

REFERENCES

Bradley, G., 2010. *Benefit Realisation Management: a practical guide to achieving benefits through change*. 2nd ed. Farnham, Surrey: Gower Publishing.

Cabinet Office, 2011. *Managing Successful Programmes*. 4th ed. London: TSO.

Jenner, S., 2012. *Managing Benefits: optimizing the return from investments*. London: APMG-International, TSO.

See also:

Knowledge Component 6.2: Assessing and managing the risks of change

Knowledge Area 7: Change Readiness, Planning and Measurement

Knowledge Component 11.5: Embedding change

Knowledge Component 3.4:
Supporting benefits realization

Measuring, monitoring and reporting benefits realization

'The success ratio of projects has not increased in fifteen years – for full delivery of benefits the success figure is still around 5%.'

Capability Management

DEFINITION

The process of supporting, managing and facilitating the realization of benefits from a change initiative is a thread that runs across all projects, programmes, and portfolios. It includes measuring, tracking and controlling both benefits and the negative effects of change.

EXPLANATION

Effective change managers play a central role in monitoring, managing and helping business managers to achieve the benefits arising from the investment in change. They work closely with programme and project managers, together with specialists and business managers to ensure that appropriate processes and systems are established for measurement, monitoring and reporting. This includes:

- Baselining all identified benefits and negative effects;

- Tracking the realization of the benefits and negative effects;

- Regularly reporting on the realization of the benefits and negative effects;

- Intervening as appropriate when benefits are not matching the plan; and

- Reviewing the overall effectiveness of benefit management and realization, including post-implementation.

Ideally, these actions are built in to the implementation plan and are an integral part of executing the project.

There is a strong link between measuring, tracking and reporting benefits and measuring and reporting change progress and effectiveness.

KNOWLEDGE

The knowledge expected of an effective Change Manager is:

1. The path from enabling changes through 'intermediate benefits' to 'end benefits'.

2. The links between the project plan or programme delivery plan and the planned benefits.

3. Methods and techniques for:

   - Baselining, measuring and tracking benefits including quantitative and qualitative measures, proxy indicators, performance assessment, audit and survey;
   - Identifying new and unexpected benefits or negative effects that might emerge;
   - Reporting benefits achievement, for example by using dashboards, normalized scales, graphical representations (such as a benefits map) and status indication (such as 'red – amber – green' (RAG).

4. When to intervene and escalate changed benefits, to forecast failure to achieve planned benefits or provide additional help to business managers to realize benefits.

REFERENCES

Jenner, S., 2012, *Managing Benefits: optimizing the return from investments.* London: APMG-International, TSO. pp.129–137.

See also:

Knowledge Area 4: Stakeholder Strategy

Knowledge Area 5: Communication and Engagement

Knowledge Component 7.4: Measuring change effectiveness

Knowledge Component 8.3: Change planning and scheduling

Knowledge Component 8.4: Executing change within a project framework

Knowledge Area 9.3: Behavioural change and coaching

Knowledge Component 11.5: Embedding change

Knowledge Area 4: Stakeholder Strategy
How to identify and engage stakeholders

BACKGROUND

A stakeholder is defined as 'any individual, group or organization that can affect, be affected by, or perceive itself to be affected by a change initiative' (Cabinet Office, 2011). A stakeholder can be internal or external to the organization. The effect on, or by, stakeholders can be positive, negative or neutral. Stakeholders are key to identifying problems that the change initiative should solve. Different stakeholders and groups view change from different perspectives. A detailed analysis of stakeholder needs, issues and priorities for change provides essential input to the change management plan.

Effective change managers play a key role alongside programme and project managers in leading, facilitating and co-ordinating engagement with stakeholders through the full lifecycle of change. This involves:

- Early and ongoing identification and categorization of key stakeholders;

- Analysis of their position and attitudes in relation to the change;

- Development of strategies and plans for engagement and communication (including review and feedback); and

- Managing and 'mobilizing' stakeholder participation in the change initiative.

KNOWLEDGE COMPONENTS

These Knowledge Components are essential to successful stakeholder strategy:

1. Identifying and segmenting stakeholders

2. Stakeholder mapping and strategy

3. Managing relationships and mobilizing stakeholders

STAKEHOLDER STRATEGY IN PRACTICE

Effective change managers ensure early and sustained engagement with key stakeholders in a change initiative, from both within and outside the organization. Using a variety of engagement and communications methods they work closely with programme and project managers, specialists and business managers to identify stakeholders who have an interest or some influence over the change. Through careful listening and an understanding of the nature and culture of the organization, effective change managers contribute to the mapping and analysis of stakeholders in a variety of ways, helping to build a strategy, together with profiles and plans for engaging with them. Effective change managers work hard to build effective stakeholder relationships, creating motivation and a desire to take action in support of the changes.

HOW THIS KNOWLEDGE AREA SUPPORTS
THE CMI CHANGE MANAGEMENT PRACTITIONER COMPETENCIES

Related Change Manager Practitioner Competencies	4.1 Identifying and segmenting stakeholders	4.2 Stakeholder mapping and strategy	4.3 Managing relationships and mobilizing stakeholders
Strategic Thinking	O	O	O
Thinking & Judgement		O	O
Influencing Others	O	O	O
Coaching for Change	O		O
Project Management	O	O	O
Communication Skills	O	O	O
Specialist Expertise – Learning & Development	O	O	O
Specialist Expertise – Communication	O	O	O

KEY REFERENCES FOR THIS KNOWLEDGE AREA

Bryson, J.M., 2003. *What To Do When Stakeholders Matter: a guide to stakeholder identification and analysis techniques.* [pdf] Available at: <http://www.governat. eu/files/files/pb_bryson_stakeholder_identification.pdf> [Accessed 25 September 2013].

Cabinet Office, 2011. *Managing Successful Programmes.* 4th ed. London: TSO.

Knowledge Component 4.1:
Identifying and segmenting stakeholders

Knowing who is interested in or can influence the change

'Find the appropriate balance of competing claims by various groups of stakeholders. All claims deserve consideration but some claims are more important than others.'

Warren Bennis

DEFINITION

Identifying and segmenting stakeholders is the process of discovering the stakeholders in an organization's change initiative and of classifying them into meaningful groupings to engage or communicate with.

EXPLANATION

For change to be successful in organizations, early and sustained engagement with stakeholders is essential. This means involving individuals, groups and organizations who have an interest in, or some influence over, the change. Stakeholders can include both internal and external interests and influences. The objective is to get the maximum possible agreement to, and support for change.

Effective change managers recognize that power and influence is not the preserve of leaders and managers but can be evident in many different areas and levels of an organization. A wide variety of stakeholder's views, interests and priorities need to be sought, listened to and understood. It is important therefore to identify and understand the relative power and influence of different stakeholders at the very beginning of a change process. Engagement should be timely, appropriate and focused on raising awareness of change and discovering real needs and concerns.

The way organizations work – their prevailing cultures and assumptions – influences the selection of the approach to change and to stakeholder engagement (Morgan 1986). When initially identifying stakeholders, a key factor is the creation the vision statement (or equivalent expression of purpose or goals) for the change initiative. At this time, effective change managers work closely with programme and project managers, and with managers and staff at all levels within an organization.

See also:

Knowledge
Component 2.4:
Developing vision

Knowledge
Component 7.1:
Building individual
motivation to change

Knowledge
Component 7.2:
Planning for
resistance

KNOWLEDGE

The knowledge expected of an effective Change Manager is:

1. Roles, processes, methods and techniques for initial and ongoing identification of, and appropriate engagement with, an organization's stakeholders, including reviews and updates of relevant information.

2. Methods and techniques for segmenting, categorizing and prioritizing stakeholders' needs, interests and concerns.

3. How to use the results of this analysis to prepare for stakeholder mapping.

REFERENCES

Bryson, J.M., 2003. *What To Do When Stakeholders Matter: a guide to stakeholder identification and analysis techniques.* [pdf] Available at: <http://www.governat. eu/files/files/pb_bryson_stakeholder_identification.pdf> [Accessed 25 September 2013].

Cabinet Office, 2011. *Managing Successful Programmes.* 4th ed. London: TSO.

Egan, G., 1994. *Working the Shadow Side: a guide to positive behind-the-scenes management.* San Francisco, CA: Jossey-Bass Management.

French, J.R.P. and Raven, B., 1959. The bases of social power. In: D. Cartwright and A. Zander, eds., 1968. *Group dynamics.* 3rd ed. New York, NY: Harper & Row.

Morgan, G., 2006. *Images of Organization.* 4th ed. London: Sage.

Knowledge Component 4.2:
Stakeholder mapping and strategy

Developing strategies for engaging with stakeholders

'In human systems, there are forces at play and generally these forces can be identified when you look at where the various stakeholders are sitting in relationship to the changes envisaged.'

Kurt Lewin

DEFINITION

Stakeholder mapping is used to analyse the stakeholders identified in the change initiative to determine how best to manage communications with them. This includes the form of the communication and level of stakeholder involvement. The results of stakeholder mapping provide essential input to the development of the change initiative's stakeholder strategy (what and how) and communications plan (when and who).

EXPLANATION

Mapping allows stakeholders to be analysed from a variety of different perspectives, including levels of power, energy, interest and commitment to the change. It also identifies:

- Levels of trust and agreement between the change effort and each stakeholder;

- The wants and needs of different communities of interest; and

- Relationships among stakeholders.

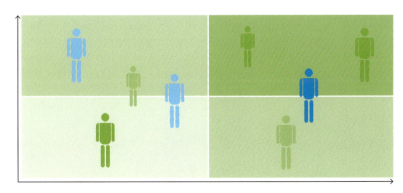

Effective change managers know that the results of these analyses can be used not only to determine stakeholders' attitudes and responses to the change but also to help to establish their form of involvement (roles and responsibilities), and the levels of engagement required with them. Mapping also enables analysis of key relationships among the different stakeholders, and among individuals, groups and organizations. Effective change managers also know that this information is an essential input into the creation of the stakeholder engagement strategy for a change initiative and the creation of the communications plan.

See also:

Knowledge Component 5.4: Planning communications

Knowledge Component 8.1: Change within project governance structures

KNOWLEDGE

The knowledge expected of an effective Change Manager is:

1. Processes, methods and techniques for mapping and analysing stakeholders from a variety of different perspectives (such as energy and commitment, impact and influence, and trust and agreement).

2. Methods and tools to map and analyse relationships between stakeholders.

3. The change roles and responsibilities (and authority) that key stakeholders may be required to adopt.

4. Stakeholder information capture and profiling techniques.

5. The purpose and content of a stakeholder engagement strategy and how this helps define appropriate engagement strategies and plans for different stakeholders.

REFERENCES

APMG-International, 2013. *Change Management Practitioner Handbook. Version 1.5.* High Wycombe, Buckinghamshire: APMG-International. Section 4.

Bryson, J.M., 2003. *What To Do When Stakeholders Matter: a guide to stakeholder identification and analysis techniques.* [pdf] Available at: <http://www.governat. eu/files/files/pb_bryson_stakeholder_identification.pdf> [Accessed 25 September 2013].

Mitchell, R.K., Agle, B.R. and Wood, D.J., 1997. Toward a Theory of Stakeholder Identification and Salience: defining the principle of who and what really counts. *Academy of Management Review,* 22(4), pp.853–888.

Reed, M.S. et al., 2009. Who's In and Why? A typology of stakeholder analysis methods for natural resource management. *Journal of Environmental Management,* 90, pp.1933–1949.

Knowledge Component 4.3: Managing relationships and mobilizing stakeholders

Securing commitment to action

'Leaders must wake people out of inertia. They must get people excited about something they've never seen before, something that does not yet exist.'

Rosabeth Moss Kanter

DEFINITION

The process of achieving and sustaining the engagement and active participation of stakeholders and stakeholder groups throughout a change initiative to ensure its long-term success.

EXPLANATION

From the beginning of a change initiative, the challenge is to achieve and sustain the engagement of stakeholders at the appropriate level. Methods and approaches drawn from public relations and marketing environments can provide a valuable additional toolkit for building the stakeholder relationships needed, for creating motivation and persuading people to act. As the change initiative progresses through its stages, continuous and effective engagement, combined with inspired and motivational leadership, is especially important. This is particularly important in the 'sticky moments in the middle of change' (Kanter, 2002). At all stages of a change initiative, effective change managers understand the need to be creative as well as consistent in developing the active involvement and building the commitment of all key stakeholders.

Effective change managers also understand the importance of 'moving' people in terms of their awareness, knowledge, active support or commitment to the change. This requires an early focus on resistance to change, allowing sufficient time and energy to address people's anxieties and concerns.

Effective change managers achieve this by:

- Seeking stakeholder opinion on the change and how it will affect them, their experience, team, business function(s) and relationships, building trust and confidence;

- Listening carefully to stakeholder interests, needs and concerns and responding openly and honestly to questions about the change and its impact;

- Making use of available communications technologies (including intranet, micro-sites, collaboration tools) to encourage dialogue, and to facilitate the sharing of ideas and information;

- Identifying and engaging with opinion leaders – those who have power or influence over others – and making them advocates (sometimes called 'champions') reducing the influence of those who do not support change; and

- Using appropriate tools to 'mobilize' stakeholders through stimulating their interest and creating a desire to take positive action.

See also:

Knowledge Component 1.2: Change and the individual

Knowledge Component 1.3: Change and the organization

Knowledge Area 5: Communication and Engagement

Knowledge Component 7.1: Building individual motivation to change

Knowledge Component 7.3: Planning for resistance

KNOWLEDGE

The knowledge expected of an effective Change Manager is:

1. Methods, approaches and concepts for:

   - Public relations to promote effective two-way dialogue with stakeholders;

   - Building and sustaining relationships with stakeholders to increase trust and confidence over time; and

   - Taking people though the steps of a typical 'sales engagement' (for example the five stage 'attention, interest, desire, action and satisfaction' (AIDAS) tool used in marketing).

2. Factors that influence stakeholder involvement in the change process, such as:

   - Human resources available to support the change (including the change team, corporate services, line managers and staff);

   - Motivation and resistance of the people affected;

   - 'Quick wins' as first action steps to energize stakeholders and stimulate participation; and

   - Frequency of stakeholder feedback, both formal (for example in focus groups) and informal ('corridor conversations').

3. Identifying power sources in the organization, calculating where power may transfer to due to the change and how such power sources and shifts affect the organization throughout the change.

REFERENCES

Aldrich, J., 2012. *Using PR Principles to Improve your Organizational Change Management Initiative.* [online] Available at: <http://panorama-consulting.com/using-pr-principles-to-improve-your-organizational-change-management-initiative> [Accessed 16 June 2013].

APMG-International, 2013. *Change Management Practitioner Handbook.* Version 1.5. High Wycombe, Buckinghamshire: APMG-International. Section 4.

Fred, C., 2012. Power and Leadership: an influence process. *International Journal of Management, Business and Administration,* 15(1). [pdf] Available at: <http://www.nationalforum.com/Electronic%20Journal%20Volumes/Lunenburg,%20Fred%20C%20Power%20and%20Leadership-An%20Influence%20Process%20IJMBA%20V15%20N1%202012.pdf> [Accessed 25 September 2013].

Lee, B., 1998. *The Power Principle: influence with honor.* New York, NY: Fireside.

Rogers, E.M., 2003. *Diffusion of Innovations.* 5th ed. New York, NY: Free Press.

Zimmerman, A. and Maenning, C., 2007. *Mainstreaming Participation: multi-stakeholder management, tools for stakeholder analysis, 10 building blocks for designing participatory systems of cooperation.* [pdf] (Deutsche Gesellschaft for Technische Zusammenarbeit (GTZ)) Available at: <http://www.fsnnetwork.org/sites/default/files/en-svmp-instrumente-akteuersanalyse.pdf> [Accessed 16 June 2013].

The Change Management Institute

Knowledge Area 5: Communication and Engagement

Communicating change effectively

BACKGROUND

Communication and engagement are at the heart of any successful change initiative. Thorough plans for implementing change may well be in place, but ultimately it is the people impacted by the change who need to be prepared to accept it and adopt new ways of doing things. If they have not received sufficient communications or had opportunities to be actively engaged in the process, there will be much greater resistance and change will not occur.

Effective change managers:

- Build awareness of the need for change;

- Help to develop a common understanding among the stakeholders of what is required; and

- Gain commitment to make change happen and maintain this level of commitment throughout the change initiative.

If there are communications specialists within an organization the change manager can work closely with them to develop appropriate communication channels. A well thought out and structured approach to planning effective communications and engagement ensures the right information reaches the right people, at the right time, in an efficient and appropriate way. Communication cannot be just one-way of course. A change manager must understand the levels of engagement and commitment required from people along the way and plan for the necessary interventions to ensure lasting change can occur.

KNOWLEDGE COMPONENTS

These Knowledge Components are essential for successful communication and engagement:

1. Theory of effective communicating

2. Communicating change

3. Communication channels

4. Planning communications

COMMUNICATION AND ENGAGEMENT IN PRACTICE

Effective change managers are proactive about maintaining high-levels of communication throughout the change initiative. They identify the people involved and impacted by the change. They consider how communication messages could be perceived by others, what their concerns are and the questions they might have. Change managers invest time and effort to seek advice from other experts and find the most appropriate ways to communicate and engage with people.

Change managers actively network and talk to people to gather more input and feedback. They are prepared to respond to feedback and adapt their approach if necessary. They are aware of organizational hierarchies and the importance of involving the right people in communication activities.

They invest time in planning communication activities to ensure consistent and timely communication throughout the change initiative.

HOW THIS KNOWLEDGE AREA SUPPORTS
THE CMI CHANGE MANAGEMENT PRACTITIONER COMPETENCIES

Related Change Manager Practitioner Competencies	5.1 Theory of effective communicating	5.2 Communicating change	5.3 Communication channels	5.4 Planning communications
Facilitating Change	O	O		O
Strategic Thinking	O	O	O	
Influencing Others	O	O	O	O
Coaching for Change	O	O		
Project Management			O	
Communication Skills	O	O	O	O
Specialist Expertise – Communication	O	O	O	O

KEY REFERENCES FOR THIS KNOWLEDGE AREA

Balogun, J. and Hailey, V.H., 2008. *Exploring Strategic Change.* 3rd ed. Harlow, Essex: Pearson Education.

Prosci, 2012. *Best Practices in Change Management,* Loveland, CO: Prosci. pp.78–88.

Smythe, J., 2007. *The CEO – Chief Engagement Officer: turning hierarchy upside down to drive performance.* Aldershot, Hampshire: Gower Publishing.

Knowledge Component 5.1:
Theory of effective communicating

Designing targeted, tailored communications

'The single biggest problem in communication is the illusion that it has taken place.'

George Bernard Shaw

DEFINITION

Organizational communication is defined as 'the sending and receiving of messages among inter-related individuals within a particular environment or setting, to achieve individual and common goals' (Hahn, Lippert and Paynton, 2011). This indicates that successful communication is more than the mere transmission of messages. The message needs to be received and interpreted in the way it was intended, which in turn leads to a change in the behaviour or thinking of those at the receiving end.

EXPLANATION

Effective change managers appreciate that there are many potential barriers to successful communication in organizations and that messages can easily be misinterpreted. Too much information may be overlooked or become overwhelming. Too little information causes frustration and anxiety, which can lead to greater resistance. Environments with greater hierarchy and complex political dynamics can hinder the easy flow and exchange of information.

Effective change managers develop strategies to take account of diverse groups of people with different perceptions and expectations in order to minimize the potential pitfalls of communication. Working closely with other staff in change roles – such as the sponsor, and the programme and project managers – they make sure the flow of information is timely and tailor the messages to be relevant and shaped for the different audiences. People prefer different ways of processing information, so the same messages need to be conveyed in different formats and styles. Effective communications approaches also incorporate feedback loops, so people can clarify any misunderstandings.

See also:

Knowledge Component 1.3: Change and the organization

Knowledge Component 12.4: Effective influence

KNOWLEDGE

The knowledge expected of an effective Change Manager is:

1. Basic models of communication theory (see Shannon and Weaver), including different communication styles and the ways people process information.

2. Overcoming barriers to successful communication (for example cultural differences, boundaries due to organizational structures, and the lack of subject knowledge).

3. Gathering relevant data about the different ways of communicating within an organization, including:

   • Verbal and written forms of communication;
   • Non-verbal (such as body language and gestures);
   • Symbolic means (such as rituals); and
   • Narrative/storytelling.

4. Applying different approaches to communication:

   • Monologic (one-way);
   • Dialogic (two-way); and
   • Participatory.

5. How cognitive biases lead to filtering of the communication received.

6. Monitoring and evaluating the effectiveness of communications approaches.

REFERENCES

APMG-International, 2013. *Change Management Practitioner Handbook.* Version 1.5. High Wycombe, Buckinghamshire: APMG-International. Section 3.

Blundel, R., Ippolito, K. and Donnarumma, D., 2008. *Effective Organisational Communication.* 3rd ed. Harlow, Essex: Pearson Education.

Fiske, J., 1996. *Introduction to Communication Studies.* 2nd ed. London: Routledge. pp.1–38.

Goodman, J. and Truss, C., 2004. *The Medium and the Message: communicating effectively during a major change initiative. Journal of Change Management,* 4(3), pp.217–228.

Hahn, L.K., Lippert L., and Paynton S., 2011. *Survey of Communication Study.* [ebook] Available at: <http://en.wikibooks.org/wiki/Survey_of_Communication_Study/Chapter_11_-_Organizational_Communication> [Accessed 22 July 2013]. Chapter 11

Kahneman, D., 2012. *Thinking Fast and Slow.* London: Penguin. pp.19–97.

Shannon, C.E. and Weaver, W., 1949. *The Mathematical Theory of Communication.* Champaign, IL: University of Illinois Press.

Verma, V.K., 1996. *Human Resource Skills for the Project Manager: the human aspects of project management.* Volume 2. Sylva, NC: Project Management Institute. pp.15–54.

Knowledge Component 5.2: Communicating change

Choosing the right levels and types of communication

'To effectively communicate, we must realize that we are all different in the way we perceive the world and use this understanding as a guide to our communications with others.'

Tony Robbins

DEFINITION

The process of creating flow and exchange of information to foster an environment in which people are engaged and committed to making the change initiative successful.

EXPLANATION

Any change initiative requires different levels of communication and engagement at different points of the journey. Typically, the earlier phases involve gathering information, exploring options and 'selling' the ideas to gain buy-in and build momentum for the change. As change progresses, regular updates on progress and additional support are more likely to be required to help reduce anxiety and build enthusiasm instead. Effective change managers acknowledge people's emotions and, anticipating their needs, they can prepare relevant and timely interventions. In order to build commitment for the change initiative it is important to engage and motivate these people. Where possible, change managers work closely with internal communications specialists to develop a suitable narrative and key messages.

Effective change managers:

- Use their judgement and skills in applying the right channels and types of communication, depending on the nature of the change and the needs of the audience. This includes working with change leaders to ensure that desired styles of communication and of leadership are aligned;

- Appreciate that, for building support, having the right people to deliver the message is just as important as using the right medium;

- Remain focused on communicating and engaging with different stakeholders throughout the change initiative;

- Challenge assumptions about 'the way we do things around here' and seek views from different perspectives; and

- Use feedback loops to foster a climate of trust and to provide valuable feedback on the effectiveness of the communications approaches used.

See also:

Knowledge Component 1.5: Organizational culture and change

Knowledge Component 2.4: Developing vision

Knowledge Component 4.3: Managing relationships and mobilizing stakeholders

KNOWLEDGE

The knowledge expected of an effective Change Manager is:

1. Understanding of organizational cultures and the nature of different types of change.

2. Using appropriate language to improve communication and engagement:

   - Making key messages relevant for the different interest groups across the organization;
   - Phrasing key messages so that they gain and hold attention;
   - Engaging people with rational logic as well as emotionally (for example by using metaphors and narrative/storytelling); and
   - Repeating communication to ensure people 'hear'.

3. The emotional impact of change on the people affected.

4. Concepts of 'relationship marketing' for engaging with different groups of stakeholders.

5. Methods for measuring effectiveness of change interventions.

REFERENCES

Balogun, J. and Hailey, V.H., 2008. *Exploring Strategic Change.* 3rd ed. Harlow, Essex: Pearson Education.

Denning, S., 2005. *The Leader's Guide to Storytelling: mastering the art and discipline of business narrative.* San Francisco, CA: Wiley.

Frahm, J. and Brown, K., 2006. Developing Communicative Competencies for a Learning Organization. *Journal of Management Development*, 25(3), pp.201–212

Kanter, R.M., 2003. *Leadership for Change: Enduring Skills for Change Masters (Harvard Business Review Case Study,* 9-304-062). [pdf] Available at: <http://hbr.org/product/leadership-for-change-enduring-skills-for-change-m/an/304062-PDF-ENG> [Accessed 20 July 2013]

Owen, N., 2002. *The Magic of Metaphor.* Carmarthen, Wales: Crown House Publishing.

Parkin, M., 2010. *Tales for Change: using storytelling to develop people and organizations.* 2nd ed. London: Kogan Page.

Smythe, J., 2007. *The CEO – Chief Engagement Officer: turning hierarchy upside down to drive performance.* Aldershot, Hampshire: Gower Publishing.

Knowledge Component 5.3: Communication channels

Matching communication to people's needs

'You can have brilliant ideas, but if you can't get them across, your ideas won't get you anywhere.'

Lee Iacocca

DEFINITION

Communication channels are different ways of exchanging ideas and information across the organization. Using them effectively is critical for achieving higher levels of engagement and overcoming the inevitable challenges that will arise during any change initiative.

EXPLANATION

Traditional attitudes to communicating change in organizations have tended to be one-directional. The message is sent but there is little opportunity for people at the receiving end to ask questions, clarify meaning, provide feedback or input and exchange ideas. This may be sufficient if the purpose is simply to relay information. However, approaches that enable multi-directional flow and exchange of information help people to become actively involved in making change happen. This becomes even more important during more complex, emergent change.

Effective change managers are skilled in finding suitable ways to meet the communication needs of the diverse groups of people involved in the change, using appropriate communication throughout the change initiative.

This means adopting a variety of approaches for achieving different outcomes, such as:

- Selling ideas to get greater buy-in for change, as opposed to simply relaying information;

- Seeking views, opinions and feedback to develop ideas further and measuring effectiveness of change interventions;

- Getting people involved in actively championing the change; and

- Having others collaborate to propose solutions and solve problems.

It is important to consider the use of social media and modern collaboration tools for managing change. They are a potentially valuable addition to communication channels, helping to achieve acceptance of change and build critical mass. When change managers make use of the wide range of the available methods, tools and technologies, they have much greater choice and flexibility in finding suitable ways to engage people and bring about successful change.

See also:

Knowledge Component 4.3: Managing relationships and mobilizing stakeholders

Knowledge Component 7.4: Measuring change effectiveness

KNOWLEDGE

The knowledge expected of an effective Change Manager is:

1. Concepts of 'relationship marketing'.

2. Advantages and disadvantages of:

   - 'Lean' and 'rich' communication channels;
   - Participatory and non-participatory methods; and
   - 'Push and pull' (self-service) channels.

3. Opportunities and risks of using social media, including policy constraints and potential pitfalls.

4. Purposes of the available communication channels, and how and when to use them.

5. Suitable ways of measuring the effectiveness of the various channels used and appropriate timing of each measurement.

REFERENCES

Adair, J., 2009. *Effective Communication: the most important management skill of all.* London: Pan Books.

Balogun, J. and Hailey, V.H., 2008. *Exploring Strategic Change.* 3rd ed. Harlow, Essex: Pearson Education.

Blundel, R., Ippolito, K. and Donnarumma, D., 2008. *Effective Organisational Communication.* 3rd ed. Harlow, Essex: Pearson Education.

Fill, C. and Jamieson, B., 2006. *Marketing Communications.* [ebook] Edinburgh: Edinburgh Business School. Available through: Heriot-Watt University library website <http://www.coursewebsites.ebsglobal.net> [Accessed 15 July 2013].

Frahm, J. and Brown, K., 2006. Developing Communicative Competencies for a Learning Organization. *Journal of Management Development*, 25(3), pp.201–212.

Larkin, T.J. and Larkin, S., 1994. *Communicating Change.* New York, NY: McGraw Hill.

Knowledge Component 5.4:
Planning communications

Developing a communications plan

'Let our advance worrying become advance thinking and planning.'
Winston Churchill

DEFINITION

A communications plan describes what will be communicated when, by whom and how. The plan is developed and used as early as possible and maintained throughout a change initiative.

EXPLANATION

Effective communication is such a critical aspect of managing change that it needs careful consideration and thorough planning. Change managers consider the aims of the change initiative, understand the terrain and culture within which change is taking place, and use the information gathered from thorough stakeholder analysis.

Effective change managers work closely with other change roles to design suitable interventions that will move people from where they are at – in terms of their attitude towards the change – to where they need to be for the change to occur. This might involve:

- Providing information to raise their awareness of the changes planned;

- Raising their level of understanding through discussion and meaningful dialogue;

- Reducing resistance to change or gaining a more favourable response through dialogue and greater involvement; or

- Actively participating and championing the change initiative through increased responsibility and sense of accountability.

Based on the strategy, appropriate communication interventions are planned – working out *what* is being communicated when, by whom and how – to ensure effective communications occur in a consistent and structured way.

Depending on the scale of the change initiative, a large number of people may need to be involved in developing the communications plan. For example, if the change impacts people's jobs or working contracts, specialist input from legal and human resource areas is required.

As with any plan, it is important to review the effectiveness of the communications plan. Are the planned activities having the desired effect? What is working, what is not? Regularly reviewing the effectiveness of communications during the change process allows useful lessons to be incorporated into subsequent activities in the plan.

See also:

Knowledge Component 4.2: Stakeholder mapping and strategy

Knowledge Component 13.1: The Change Manager and Human Resources

KNOWLEDGE

The knowledge expected of an effective Change Manager is:

1. The purpose of the communications plan.

2. Taking the key steps for developing a communications plan, including identifying the main components of this plan.

3. Selecting the right people to deliver key messages while overcoming obstacles, such as boundaries due to organizational hierarchies, or too limited types of channels available).

4. How to develop key messages for the selected people, communicate these messages and sustain them.

5. Measuring the effectiveness of the communication plan.

REFERENCES

Balogun, J. and Hailey, V.H., 2008. *Exploring Strategic Change*. 3rd ed. Harlow, Essex: Pearson Education.

Cabinet Office, 2011. *Managing Successful Programmes*. 4th ed. London: TSO.

Project Management Institute, 2013. *A Guide to the Project Management Body of Knowledge (PMBOK® Guide)*. 5th ed. Newtown Square, PA: The Project Management Institute.

Smythe, J., 2007. *The CEO – Chief Engagement Officer: turning hierarchy upside down to drive performance*. Aldershot, Hampshire: Gower Publishing.

Wideman, M., 2010. *Guide on Communications Planning*. [online] Available at: <http://www.maxwideman.com/guests/short_guides/plan.htm> [Accessed 20 July 2013].

Knowledge Area 6: Change Impact

Assessing change impact and progress

BACKGROUND

When change is planned in an organization it is critical to understand the full implications and potential impacts – both positive and negative – that the change might have. Change always has some degree of impact on individuals, teams, functions/business units and the organization as a whole, as well as on third parties outside of the organization. These impacts on external parties might have adverse implications for the organization.

Change can also create great disturbance and turbulence in an organization, and care is needed to balance 'managing the change' with the ongoing task of 'managing the business'.

Identifying and analysing the impact of change enables effective initial planning and preparation, helping to avoid or at least minimize the disruptive effects of implementation on the organization's business activities. It also enables potential risks and problem-areas to be identified before they arise. Effective change managers ensure that, during the change, appropriate business continuity plans (and, if needed, contingency plans) are in place. This involves identifying which processes and functions are most critical to recover should things go wrong. Assessing impact in this way also provides a valuable framework for project planning and risk management within a change initiative.

KNOWLEDGE COMPONENTS

These Knowledge Components are essential to effective assessment of the impact of change:

1. Assessing the impact of change
2. Assessing and managing the risks of change
3. Business continuity and contingency during change

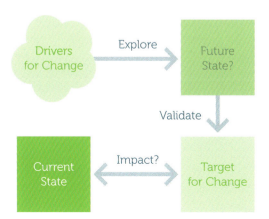

CHANGE IMPACT IN PRACTICE

Effective change managers work closely with business managers in the early stages of a change initiative to identify the full implications and potential impacts of change (including risks and opportunities) on current business and its people. This will determine how change will affect achievement of strategic goals and targets, business and operational functions, teams and staff, including existing roles, skills and capabilities. Change managers also work alongside programme and project managers, risk management specialists and business managers to establish effective governance arrangements that reflect the need to manage risks across the change management and programme/project management environments. They also play an active role in contributing to risk identification and management (including both risks to effective delivery of change and realization of benefits) as well as co-ordinating the input of key stakeholders.

Change managers also work with business managers to minimize disruption to an organization's 'business-as-usual' environment.

HOW THIS KNOWLEDGE AREA SUPPORTS
THE CMI CHANGE MANAGEMENT PRACTITIONER COMPETENCIES

Related Change Manager Practitioner Competencies	6.1 Assessing the impact of change	6.2 Assessing and managing the risks of change	6.3 Business continuity and contingency during change
Facilitating Change	O	O	O
Strategic Thinking	O	O	O
Thinking & Judgement	O	O	O
Influencing Others	O	O	O
Coaching for Change	O	O	O
Communication Skills	O		
Specialist Expertise – Learning & Development	O	O	
Specialist Expertise – Communication	O	O	

KEY REFERENCES FOR THIS KNOWLEDGE AREA

Cabinet Office, 2011. *Managing Successful Programmes*. 4th ed. London: TSO.

Cabinet Office, 2011. *Management of Portfolios*. London: TSO.

Project Management Institute, 2013. *A Guide to the Project Management Body of Knowledge (PMBOK® Guide)*. 5th ed. Newtown Square, PA: The Project Management Institute.

Knowledge Component 6.1:
Assessing the impact of change

Understanding the implications and impact of change

'Identifying the potential consequences of a change or estimating what needs to be modified to accomplish a change.'

Bohner and Arnold

DEFINITION

Change impact assessment is the process which analyses the impacts and implications of a change initiative on all aspects of the business, its operations and its people, as the basis for decision-making and planning for a change initiative.

EXPLANATION

Once the change has been properly defined it is necessary to conduct a full assessment of its impact. In carrying out an impact analysis, effective change managers seek to ensure that detailed planning for the change initiative takes full account of the implications and potential impacts of change. This includes assessing all risks and opportunities affecting the business and its people.

This places impact analysis at the heart of decision-making for the change initiative. The results and insights gained from the impact analysis may have a bearing on whether and how the change will proceed. A change manager often advises on how impact can be managed or mitigated to enable change to happen. Change can impact on some or all aspects of an organization's 'systems' and 'sub-systems' (McKinsey's '7-S framework'; and Pascale, 1990). This may include impacts on people, processes, technologies, infrastructure, culture (official and unofficial), work practices and styles. Impact analysis is closely aligned to other analytical tools, including investment appraisal or prioritization, risk analysis and stakeholder analysis.

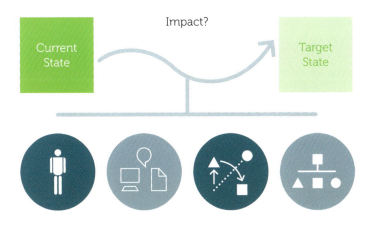

Effective change managers understand that change will impact on an organization's systems and sub-systems. This needs to be thoroughly assessed by working with the business areas to determine the specific impact and costs of change on:

- Achievements of an organization's strategic objectives and performance targets (including the key performance indicators or balanced scorecard);

- Organizational structures and culture (including which departments and divisions will be impacted or changed and the nature or degree of impact);

- Business and operational functions, teams and staff (including existing roles, skills and capabilities); and

- Customers, business partners and service providers, who may be directly or indirectly impacted.

This information is essential for guiding decision-makers during the evaluation of the results of impact analysis when planning, preparing for and implementing the change initiative.

See also:

Knowledge Component 2.1: Aligning change with strategy

Knowledge Component 2.3: Change definition

Knowledge Area 4: Stakeholder Strategy

Knowledge Component 8.5: Transitioning to the business

KNOWLEDGE

The knowledge expected of an effective Change Manager is:

1. Methods and techniques for conducting an 'impact analysis' (including 'heat maps' and process mapping) to gather relevant data and information that addresses the wider implications of change for the organization, its structure, processes, people and stakeholders.

2. Methods for evaluating and quantifying the effects and costs of managing the positive effects (benefits) on the one hand and the unexpected, negative consequences ('dis-benefits' or 'ripple-effects') of change on the other.

REFERENCES

Cabinet Office, 2011. *Management of Portfolios*. London: TSO.

Waterman, R.H. Jr., Peters, T.J. and Phillips, J.R., 1980. *Structure Is Not Organization*. [pdf] Available at: <http://www.tompeters.com/docs/Structure_Is_Not_Organization.pdf> [Accessed 25 September 2013].

Knowledge Component 6.2: Assessing and managing the risks of change

Identifying the potential threats to achievement

'The evaluation of the many risks associated with the change, including estimates of the effects on resources, effort, and schedule.'

Pfleeger and Atlee

DEFINITION

Risk assessment and risk management is the application of clearly defined techniques to identify the range of unexpected events that might disrupt the change initiative, and to quantify the magnitude and probability of their impact.

EXPLANATION

Change in an organization is, by definition, potentially disruptive to the normal 'business-as-usual' (BAU) environment. Change impacts directly on the status quo and can create a period of instability. This occurs as the organization moves from current to new ways of working, and as it adopts new systems, processes and structures.

Effective change managers know that risk management is an essential component of successful change. Change risks typically include both threats (negative impacts) and opportunities (positive impacts). A key priority is to work with programme and project managers and specialists to establish effective governance arrangements that reflect the need to manage risks across the change management and programme/project management environments.

Effective change managers know that it is critical for a change initiative to define, identify, assess and manage change risks where:

- Change has a direct or indirect impact on the operation of BAU;

- The change initiative retains a high degree of focus on achieving and embedding (sustaining) desired outcomes and on benefits realization;

- It is necessary to remove or minimize the possibility of non-adoption (or low adoption) of changes, and of reversion to the status quo;

- It is important to avoid benefit-related risks, such as a failure to deliver some or all of the forecast benefit values, or inadequate mitigation of negative effects;

- Management decision-making must be improved on all aspects of a change initiative, including establishing clear thresholds and tolerances for risk management and reporting;

- The organization must retain a balanced perspective on risk across strategic and operational levels, and across the change initiative's programmes and projects; and

- Effective engagement with stakeholders, and their participation in the change initiative, is paramount.

See also:

Knowledge Component 3.2: Benefits identification, mapping and analysis

Knowledge Component 4.3: Managing relationships and mobilizing stakeholders

Knowledge Component 5.2: Communicating change

Knowledge Component 8.2 Establishing a project

Knowledge Component 8.3 Change planning and scheduling

Knowledge Component 8.4: Executing change within a project environment

Knowledge Component 11.5 Embedding change

KNOWLEDGE

The knowledge expected of an effective Change Manager is:

1. The terms, definition and characteristics of a change risk (threat or opportunity).

2. Effective risk management governance structure (roles, responsibilities and processes).

3. Methods and techniques for identifying, capturing, analysing and mitigating/resolving risks.

4. Contents and use of a risk log for a change initiative, programme or project as a basis for management of risks, and for compiling reports for decision-makers.

REFERENCES

Cabinet Office, 2011. *Managing Successful Programmes*. 4th ed. London: TSO.

Cabinet Office, 2010. *Management of Risk: Guidance for Practitioners*. 3rd ed. London: TSO.

Project Management Institute, 2013. *A Guide to the Project Management Body of Knowledge (PMBOK® Guide)*. 5th ed. Newtown Square, PA: The Project Management Institute.

Knowledge Component 6.3:
Business continuity and contingency during change

Minimizing the effects of non-controlled change on normal business

'Planning is bringing the future into the present so that you can do something about it now.'

Alan Lakein

DEFINITION

The process of using 'change management' as a means of minimizing potential risks to business continuity as a direct consequence of a change initiative. This involves safeguarding the interests of key stakeholders, reputation, brand and value-creating activities. It involves planning for the recovery of business processes should a disruption to the business occur because of making changes.

EXPLANATION

Change can be disruptive and care needs to be taken to balance 'managing the change' with the ongoing task of 'managing the business'. Identifying and analysing the impact of change enables effective initial planning and preparation. This helps to minimize the effects of (non-controlled) change on the organization's normal business functions and activities. If the organization already has an established process for business continuity and contingency planning, the effective change manager's focus is to ensure business managers regularly review these plans against the change initiative. This helps to identify new and changed risks to business management, services or operational delivery. These may include assessing potential impacts of the change initiative on business partners, service providers, service users, customers and other external stakeholders.

It is not expected that a Change Manger will be an expert practitioner in business continuity or contingency planning. In some organizations this role may already be defined at corporate level. In this case the change manager and the corporate business continuity roles will work together to identify the potential impacts of a change initiative on business-as-usual (BAU).

Effective change managers recognize that change management and delivery plans must be based on a thorough appreciation and awareness of the potential impacts to BAU, including new and changing risks, through:

- Reviewing (or where they do not already exist, mapping) current business processes to identify 'core' business activities, functions, processes and systems, including organizational relationships, links and dependencies;

- Undertaking (and reviewing or maintaining) a high-level identification and analysis of potential impact scenarios and 'hot-spots' (critical points at which the proposed change initiative could impact on business-as-usual);

- Confirming (or reviewing existing) statements on 'normal operations';

- Capturing relevant information about the specific steps or measures required to manage or reduce the impact of change where practicable; and

- Advising business managers on new or updated contingency plans or arrangements needed to maintain business continuity through the change process.

See also:

Knowledge Component 2.5: Scenario design and testing

Knowledge Component 8.5: Transitioning to the business

KNOWLEDGE

The knowledge expected of an effective Change Manager is:

1. The principles of business continuity planning and contingency planning methods and techniques.

2. Awareness of methods and techniques for conducting a business impact analysis (BIA) to gather information about business functions processes and systems, including organizational relationships, links and dependencies, using appropriate methods, tools and techniques.

3. Using the results of a business impact analysis to identify impact 'hot-spots' where risks and issues need to be addressed as part of the change initiative, including identification of specific contingency requirements and plans to minimize disturbance to BAU.

REFERENCES

Hotchkiss, S., 2010. *Business Continuity Management: in practice.* Swindon, Wiltshire: British Computer Society.

Sterling, S. et al., The Cabinet Office 2012. *Business Continuity for Dummies.* Chichester, W Sussex: John Wiley & Sons.

Knowledge Area 7: Change Readiness, Planning and Measurement

Preparing for change

BACKGROUND

When a change initiative begins, there is a context of 'change readiness'. This includes the degree of change readiness for this – *or any* – change among all people who will receive it, and the existing level of employee engagement. Effective change managers assess these factors before change starts, influence them in a positive and appropriate manner, and continue to monitor them as the change progresses. The information gathered will often form a central part in a change manager's regular progress reporting.

Importantly, it is necessary to gauge and manage these measures at the detailed project level, as well as at the wider programme or organizational levels. This will mean ensuring that the change is aligned with:

- The strategy and mission of the organization

- The programme design, and

- The project definition.

Effective change managers are not specialists in developing formal opinion surveys. However, they do need to know how to construct and administer simple surveys and other feedback systems to support their work. They must also understand people well enough to identify the impact of various human motivations, and how these might increase or diminish change readiness or resistance.

KNOWLEDGE COMPONENTS

These Knowledge Components are essential to the successful preparation for change:

1. Building individual motivation to change

2. Building organizational readiness to change

3. Planning for resistance

4. Measuring change effectiveness

PREPARING FOR CHANGE IN PRACTICE

Effective change managers gather information regarding the organization's general readiness for change and the readiness for the specific changes in question. This is done using a blend of different approaches such as historical survey information, new surveys designed specifically for this task, interviews and workshops. Combining this with the organization's prior history of change allows change managers to build a rich picture of the current state of readiness and the likely challenges to come. Combining approaches to motivation and change resistance with knowledge of Stakeholder Strategy, Communication and Engagement, and Education and Learning Support creates a robust approach for the change initiative. Continuously 'taking the temperature' throughout by collecting both measurable results (such as surveys) and anecdotal information (such as interviews) builds a feedback system that allows the effective change manager to continuously adapt the approach to suit the situation.

**HOW THIS KNOWLEDGE AREA SUPPORTS
THE CMI CHANGE MANAGEMENT PRACTITIONER COMPETENCIES**

Related Change Manager Practitioner Competencies	7.1 Building individual motivation to change	7.2 Building organizational readiness to change	7.3 Planning for resistance	7.4 Measuring change effectiveness
Facilitating Change	O	O	O	O
Strategic Thinking		O		O
Influencing Others	O	O	O	O
Coaching for Change	O	O		
Project Management				O
Communication Skills	O	O	O	O
Specialist Expertise – Learning & Development	O	O	O	O
Specialist Expertise – Communication	O	O	O	O

KEY REFERENCES FOR THIS KNOWLEDGE AREA

Blake, I. and Bush, C., 2009. *Project Managing Change.* Harlow, Essex: Pearson Education.

Cameron, E. and Green, M., 2012. *Making Sense of Change Management: a complete guide to the models, tools and techniques of organizational change.* 3rd ed. London: Kogan Page.

Kotter, J.P. and Schlesinger, L.A., 2008. Choosing Strategies for Change. *Harvard Business Review,* July–August 2008, 86(7–8), pp.130–139.

The March 2013 issue of *Journal of Change Management* Vol.13(1) contains a number of significant articles relating to Change Readiness.

Knowledge Component 7.1:
Building individual motivation to change

Building and sustaining commitment to change

'Change is the law of life and those who look only to the past or present are certain to miss the future.'

John F Kennedy

DEFINITION

In the context of a change initiative, motivation is about winning and sustaining an interest in, and desire to make, the required changes.

EXPLANATION

Effective change managers know that a change will fail in whole or in part unless it engages the commitment and motivation of the people who must receive the change. Unless 'hearts and minds' are won over, there will be little effort to engage with the change. To achieve this, effective change managers know the importance of the emotional responses to change.

Change managers understand human drives and motivation, apply their understanding to help to build and sustain motivation for change and help their colleagues to do the same. Closely related to this Knowledge Component is the subject of identifying areas of possible resistance to change and planning for it. While building motivation and commitment is a more positive approach, proactively preparing for resistance and other challenges is also a vital part of change management.

Another key aspect of change management is to plan the 'campaign' that will win over the people who must change, overcome barriers, build trust and confidence.

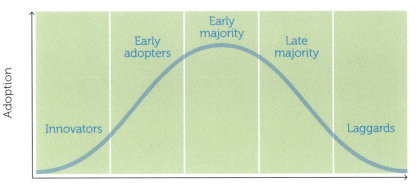

Source: Rogers (1963)

KNOWLEDGE

The knowledge expected of an effective Change Manager is:

1. Classic theories of human motivation, including:

   • Behaviourist approaches to rewards and sanctions (Maslow, McClelland, McGregor and Hertzberg), and their likely impacts on people in a change process; and
   • The 'expectancy theory' in relation to behaviourist approaches (Lunenberg, 2011).

2. Concepts of forces that are driving or resisting change (such as Edgar Schein's 'transformative change' model and Richard Beckhard's and Harris's 'change formula').

3. Positive psychological approaches (such as 'appreciative enquiry').

4. Theories of how changes spread (Rogers, 1962).

REFERENCES

Beckhard, R., 1969. *Organization Development: strategies and models*. Reading, MA: Addison-Wesley.

Cameron, E. and Green, M., 2012. *Making Sense of Change Management: a complete guide to the models, tools and techniques of organizational change*. 3rd ed. London: Kogan Page.

Chamorro-Premuzic, T., 2013. *Does Money Really Affect Motivation? A review of the research*. [online] Available at: <http://blogs.hbr.org/cs/2013/04/does_money_really_affect_motiv.html> [Accessed 15 July 2013].

Kini, T., 2003. Exploit What You Do Best. *Harvard Management Update*, August, 8(8).

Lunenberg, F., 2011. Expectancy Theory of Motivation: motivating by altering expectations. *International Journal of Management, Business and Administration*, 15(1).

McClelland, D.C., 2010. *The Achieving Society*. Staten Island, NY: Pober.

Rock, D., 2008. *SCARF: a brain-based model for collaborating with and influencing others*. [pdf] Available at: <http://www.your-brain-at-work.com/files/NLJ_SCARFUS.pdf> [Accessed 12 July 2013].

Rogers, E.M., 2003. *Diffusion of Innovations*. 5th ed. New York, NY: Free Press.

Schein, E., 1995. *Kurt Lewin's Change Theory in the Field and in the Classroom: Notes Toward a Model of Managed Learning*. [pdf] Available at: <http://www.dspace.mit.edu/bitstream/handle/1721.1/2576/SWP-3821-32871445.pdf> [Accessed 19 August 2013].

FURTHER INFORMATION

There are various excellent summaries of McClelland's theories available on the internet, including the following:

McClelland, D., [online] Available at: <http://www.mindtools.com/pages/article/human-motivation-theory.htm> [Accessed 19 July 2013] and <http://www.businessballs.com/davidmcclelland.htm> [Accessed 19 July 2013].

Knowledge Component 7.2: Building organizational readiness to change

The capability, capacity and belief to see change through

'If I keep on saying to myself that I cannot do a certain thing, it is possible that I may end by really becoming incapable of doing it. On the contrary, if I have the belief that I can do it, I shall surely acquire the capacity to do it even if I may not have it at the beginning.'

Mahatma Gandhi

DEFINITION

The process of identifying and developing the extent of the organization's readiness to change. This is not just the shared capacity and capability to support a change initiative with the required skills, experience and resources. It is also the belief in that capacity and the resolve to see it through.

EXPLANATION

These are critical success factors in change (both before and after the change) and an assessment of them is an essential element of defining and scoping a change. They are also essential factors to review as the initiative progresses.

Change readiness starts with managers of an initiative recognizing the implications of the change on the people who must receive the change. However, more mature organizations recognize the need to extend readiness across the whole organization. In mature organizations, all areas of the business should be comfortable with high degrees of constant change. Coherent management of change may be achieved across the whole organization, with centralized reporting at the highest level.

Early evaluation of organizational change readiness (or any sub-division, team or group within it) contributes to effective preparation for the change. It ensures that the organization's past experiences of change, the lessons learned, and current attitudes are reflected in the change management plan.

Strategies for preparing an organization for change include:

- Challenging existing thinking;

- Raising awareness of the need for change; and

- Addressing current and future performance issues and implications (such as peaks and troughs in workload).

Implementing complex organizational changes requires high levels of stakeholder participation and collaboration, creating additional pressures on people and resources.

Effective change managers know that a key success criterion for change in organizations is progressively to build, establish and prove change management, along with portfolio, programme and project management, as key competencies. This will be achieved through:

- A realistic assessment of an organization's change capability and capacity, including the resources (physical, financial and human) required to specify, plan, implement and embed change;

- Supporting the development of change management competence and skills across the organization;

- Ensuring skills development is an integral part of the change management plan.

See also:

Knowledge Component 8.3: Change planning and scheduling

Knowledge Component 9.1: Learning theory and skills development

Knowledge Component 9.2: Identifying and meeting learning needs

KNOWLEDGE

The knowledge expected of an effective Change Manager is:

1. Methods of assessing the factors that influence readiness for change (such as surveys, workshops and conversations). These methods include evaluating:

   - Cultural factors, values, management styles and shared perspectives;
   - Competences in change related disciplines (such as communication, learning and development), and project management;
   - Organizational policy; and
   - Lessons from past initiatives.

2. The key actions and decisions required to lay the foundations for a successful change initiative, including:

   - Building awareness of the need for change;
   - Ensuring participation and building support;
   - Assessing and developing the skills of the stakeholders;
   - Building a change team with the necessary skills and experience; and
   - Evaluating the readiness of the organization's systems and processes.

3. Ways of matching the scope and extent of the change against the types and quantity of resources needed.

4. Methods and techniques for defining the set of typical recurring actions that contribute to change readiness.

5. Approaches to training and education in change management (and related disciplines), as an integral part of the change management plan.

REFERENCES

Armenakis, A.A., Harries, S.G. and Mossholder, K.W., 1993. Creating Readiness for Organizational Change. *Human Relations,* 46(6), pp.681–703.

Change Management Institute, 2012. *Organisational Change Management Maturity.* [pdf] Available at: <https://www.change-management-institute.com/sites/default/files/CMI%20White%20Paper%2C%20Change%20Agility%20-%20Feb%202012_1.pdf> [Accessed 17 September 2013].

Harvard Business Essentials, 2003. *Managing Change and Transition. Boston, MA: Harvard Business Press. pp.17–29.*

Meyer, J.P., 2002. *Commitment to an Organizational Change: extension of a three-component model. Journal of Applied Psychology,* 87(3), pp.474–487.

Prosci, 2012. *Best Practices in Change Management,* Loveland, CO: Prosci. pp.52–53.

Weiner, B.J., 2009. A Theory of Organizational Readiness for Change. *Implementation Science, 4(67).*

Knowledge Component 7.3: Planning for resistance

Understanding that challenges are to be expected

'People don't resist change. They resist being changed.'

Peter Senge

DEFINITION

People react differently to change, however minor or rational it might seem. Some rapidly embrace it. However, some actively fight the change, either openly or quietly undermining it. Others simply refuse to engage. This is known as resistance to change. Resistance to change is normal; it should be expected and planned for.

EXPLANATION

Effective change managers prepare for resistance and challenges to change. Organizations frequently struggle with the effort required to make substantive change, finding it hard to make the case and to free the resources. Once the change has gained a foothold, a lack of initial success and a growing sense of unease can hold back momentum, making the communication of 'quick wins' especially helpful. However, resistance to change, which individuals or groups may exhibit to certain extents, offers a particular challenge, which change managers need to address.

There are many causes of resistance and it is displayed in a variety of forms, including apathy. Effective change managers understand that resistance, whatever its cause or the form it takes, shows that people are engaged and care about the situation. Highlighting genuine flaws in a change initiative – or that the change, when implemented, may have a long-term detrimental impact on everyday work – also help change managers.

The sources of resistance may include:

- The genuine rational concerns of those affected about the change;

- A lack of organizational readiness for change;

- Normal human processes of change (for example the fear of failure);

- Existing unhelpful relationships and lack of trust between general staff and management;

- Inadequate support for the change from managers and supervisors; and

- Poor sponsorship of the change, especially low visibility.

If there are different sources of resistance, then appropriate strategies for dealing with each one of them are needed. The extent and combination of these sources helps a change manager assess the likely magnitude of resistance and the effort needed to address it. This contributes to effective planning.

Effective change managers understand the importance of preparing managers and supervisors at all levels of the organization for change. Such preparation enlists their support and minimizes the negative aspects of resistance to change.

KNOWLEDGE

The knowledge expected of an effective Change Manager is:

1. The 'psychological contract', its meaning and its implications during a change.

2. Methods and approaches for:

   - Supporting business managers and supervisors (for example by coaching them and offering workshops); and
   - Identifying likely areas of resistance (especially when using surveys and workshops).

3. Causes and types of resistance to change, and symptoms to look for.

4. The parts that managers and supervisors play in creating, sustaining and overcoming resistance to change.

5. Common considerations for building a strategy (which is appropriate to the nature, speed and strategic impact of the change) to manage resistance.

6. Appropriate strategies for mitigating the common organizational challenges of building and sustaining the momentum of a change initiative (Senge et al., 1999; Kotter and Schlesinger, 2008; and Kotter, 2012).

See also:

Knowledge Component 1.2: Change and the individual

Knowledge Component 1.3: Change and the organization

Knowledge Area 4: Stakeholder Strategy

Knowledge Area 5: Communication and Engagement

Knowledge Component 6.2: Assessing and managing the risks of change

Knowledge Area 9: Education and Learning Support

Knowledge Area 11: Sustaining Systems

Knowledge Component 12.4: Effective influence

REFERENCES

Ford, J.D. and Ford, L.W., 2009. Decoding Resistance to Change. *Harvard Business Review,* April, pp.99–103.

Kanter, R.M., 2012. *Ten Reasons People Resist Change.* [online] Available at: <http://blogs.hbr.org/kanter/2012/09/ten-reasons-people-resist-chang. html> [Accessed 15 July 2013].

Kotter, J.P. and Schlesinger, L.A., 2008. Choosing Strategies for Change. *Harvard Business Review,* July–August 2008, 86(7–8), pp.130–139.

Kotter, J.P., 2012. *Leading Change.* 2nd ed. Boston, MA: Harvard Business Review Press.

Michelman, P., 2007. Overcoming Resistance to Change. *Harvard Management Update,* 12(7).

Nguyen Huy, Q., 2001. In Praise of Middle Managers. *Harvard Business Review,* September, 79(8), pp.72–78.

Prosci, 2012. *Best Practices in Change Management,* Loveland, CO: Prosci. pp.71–77, pp.90–97.

Schein, E., 1995. *Kurt Lewin's Change Theory in the Field and in the Classroom: Notes Toward a Model of Managed Learning.* [pdf] Available at: <http://www. dspace.mit.edu/bitstream/handle/1721.1/2576/SWP-3821-32871445.pdf> [Accessed 19 August 2013].

Senge, P. et al., 1999. *The Dance Of Change: the challenge of sustaining momentum in learning organizations.* London: Nicholas Brealey.

FURTHER INFORMATION

There is plenty of material on the web that is available on the concept of the Psychological Contract. One particularly helpful example is this fact sheet, which requires free registration with the UK's Chartered Institute of Personnel and Development (CIPD).

The Chartered Institute of Personnel and Development (CIPD), 2013. *The Psychological Contract.* [online] Available at: <http://www.cipd.co.uk/hr-resources/factsheets/psychological-contract.aspx> [Accessed 19 July 2013].

Knowledge Component 7.4:
Measuring change effectiveness

'Taking the temperature' and tracking progress

'There's a fundamental distinction between strategy and operational effectiveness.'

Michael Porter

DEFINITION

Change management is ultimately concerned with people, their feelings and behaviours. These are complex issues and sometimes hard to measure with complete precision. Nonetheless, gauging the effectiveness of the change strategies, both statistically and anecdotally is fundamental to successful change management.

EXPLANATION

Effective change managers build commitment among the people affected by the change; further, they identify and manage areas of resistance. To do this well, change managers periodically 'take the temperature'. In other words: they find ways to gauge the levels of readiness for change and of commitment to the change. They also recognize the importance of tracking 'hard' or 'objective' measures of change activities (such as progress with training).

Methods of collecting the information can include surveys, in various different formats, focus groups, workshops, and individual interviews. Members of the team who are supporting the change initiative (such as trainers or business analysts) can also provide useful feedback.

Each method of collecting information has advantages and disadvantages; none is ideal when used in isolation. It is usually necessary to formulate a strategy for collecting information that takes into account the practicalities of the situation and uses a blend of several different approaches. This ensures a rich and full picture of how effective the change management strategies and activities are proving.

Overall readiness for change is a critical factor in any decision to finally transition the change to the business.

See also:

Knowledge
Component 8.5:
Transitioning to
the business

Knowledge Area 10:
Facilitation

KNOWLEDGE

The knowledge expected of an effective Change Manager is:

1. Typical measures of change management effectiveness (including measures of engagement and readiness, as well as 'harder' measures such progress with training and other deliverables).

2. Methods of capturing information about readiness and engagement with change – for example one-off surveys, pulse surveys, focus groups, workshops, and individual interviews; each method including:

   - Effective use;
   - Data interpretation;
   - Ethical considerations; and
   - Typical contents (such as questions to ask).

   It also includes the advantages and disadvantages of each approach at each stage of the change initiative.

3. Ways of presenting and explaining levels of employee engagement and ways of using this as a measure of change management effectiveness.

REFERENCES

Berkowitz, B., *Conducting Focus Groups*. [online] (The Community Tool Box) Available at: <http://ctb.ku.edu/en/tablecontents/sub_section_main_1018.aspx> [Accessed 19 July 2013].

Monash University, *How to Conduct an Interview*. [online] Available at: <http://www.monash.edu.au/lls/hdr/develop/4.2.1.html> [Accessed 19 July 2013].

RMIT. *Tips on Facilitating Focus groups*. *[pdf]* Available at: *<http://*emedia.rmit.edu.au/edmag/files/ed_magazine/Facilitating_focus_groups.pdf> [Accessed 19 July 2013].

Rowan University,. *Toolkit for Conducting Focus Groups*. [pdf] Available at: <http://www.rowan.edu/colleges/chss/facultystaff/focusgrouptoolkit.pdf> [Accessed 19 July 2013].

US General Services Administration. *Basics of Survey and Question Design*. [online] Available at: <http://www.howto.gov/customer-experience/collecting-feedback/basics-of-survey-and-question-design> [Accessed 19 July 2013].

FURTHER INFORMATION

Many references for the use of surveys and focus groups can be found on commercial sites, including the following:

CFI-Knoll, 2012. *Three Keys to Successful Change Readiness Surveys*. [pdf] Available at: <http://www.cfi-knoll.com/knoll-white-papers/three-keys-to-successful-change-readiness-surveys.pdf> [Accessed 19 July 2013].

Clampitt, P.G., Berk, L.R. and Cashman, T, 2006. *Checking the Organizational Pulse*. [pdf] Available at: <http://www.imetacomm.com/otherpubs/pdf_doc_downloads/check_org_pulse_1-7.pdf> [Accessed 19 July 2013].

Simon, J.S., 1999. *How to Conduct a Focus Group*. [pdf] Available at: <http://www.tgci.com/magazine/How%20to%20Conduct%20a%20Focus%20Group.pdf> [Accessed 19 July 2013].

Survey Monkey, *SHRM Work Engagement Template*. [online] Available at: <http://www.surveymonkey.com/s/shrm-work-engagement-template> [Accessed 19 July 2013].

William Steinberg Consultants. *Survey Related Articles*. [online] Available at: <http://www.notjustsurveys.com/surveyarticles.html> [Accessed 19 July 2013].

Knowledge Area 8: Project Management

Change initiatives, projects and programmes

BACKGROUND

Project management and change management are distinct disciplines but practitioners of these disciplines must often work closely together.

In this context, project management covers the discipline of managing structured delivery initiatives, such as projects, programmes and portfolios.

There are many formalized methodologies and approaches to project and programme management. For example, PRINCE2® and PMBOK® are two of the most widely accepted and used international standards. However, many large organizations have developed their own methodologies. Often these in-house methodologies have used elements from one of the international standards. Many concepts are common across most methodologies.

Under all circumstances, effective change managers are aware of the actual project or programme methodology being used alongside, or as part of, the change initiative. The decision whether an 'agile' or a more linear 'waterfall' approach is used is particularly important. The methodology and approach may dictate how change managers go about critical activities, for example planning and delegating. This is important because change managers frequently need to budget, schedule and sequence tasks, and to ensure delivery of a complex range of outcomes.

It is important that change managers understand the work of project and programme managers well enough to work effectively alongside them and to make best use of their specialist expertise. Throughout the life of the change initiative, effective change managers work closely with project or programme managers ensuring that the two disciplines are in step, with a mutual agreement on the timing and nature of the deliverables and tasks required. This will frequently require that effective change managers brief the project or programme teams on aspects of effective change management.

KNOWLEDGE COMPONENTS

These Knowledge Components are essential to the successful interaction of change management and project management:

1. Change within project governance structures

2. Establishing a project

3. Change planning and scheduling

4. Executing change within a project environment

5. Transitioning to the business

PROJECT MANAGEMENT IN PRACTICE

Upon joining a change initiative or commencing one, effective change managers familiarize themselves with the project and programme methodologies in use. They form strong professional relationships with those responsible for 'business as usual' and with all levels of the hierarchy of portfolios, programmes and projects. During the period of establishing the project, change managers take an active part in the discussions and ensure that the change management plan has a central role in the governance and management processes. Change managers design and establish appropriate change teams. In parallel to more technical delivery plans, they develop their own plans, schedules, resource plans and budgets for change management activities.

During execution, change managers manage their teams effectively, develop and checks relevant deliverables, report progress and proactively manage risks and issues. The time for transition to the business is an especially critical time for change management. During transition, effective change managers are on the lookout for stakeholders who are struggling, possibly due to inadequate preparation or a mismatch between deliverables and expectations. An especially emotional time for some stakeholders can be the close down of replaced assets, such as buildings, systems or machinery. Effective change managers are watchful for this, and are prepared to address any issues that arise.

HOW THIS KNOWLEDGE AREA SUPPORTS
THE CMI CHANGE MANAGEMENT PRACTITIONER COMPETENCIES

Related Change Manager Practitioner Competencies	8.1 Change within project governance structures	8.2 Establishing a project	8.3 Change planning and scheduling	8.4 Executing change within a project environment	8.5 Transitioning to the business
Strategic Thinking	O	O		O	O
Thinking & Judgement	O		O		O
Coaching for Change			O		O
Project Management	O	O	O	O	O
Communication Skills				O	

KEY REFERENCES FOR THIS KNOWLEDGE AREA

Blake, I. and Bush, C., 2009. *Project Managing Change*. Harlow, Essex: Pearson Education.

Cabinet Office, 2011. *Managing Successful Programmes*. 4th ed. London: TSO.

Cabinet Office, 2009. *Managing Successful Projects with PRINCE2*. 5th ed. London: TSO.

Cabinet Office, 2011. *Management of Portfolios*. London: TSO.

DSDM Consortium, 2012. *Agile Project Management Handbook*. Version 1.1, Ashford, Kent: DSDM Consortium.

Project Management Institute, 2013. *A Guide to the Project Management Body of Knowledge (PMBOK® Guide)*. 5th ed. Newtown Square, PA: The Project Management Institute.

Project Management Institute, 2013. *The Standard for Program Management*. 3rd ed. Newtown Square, PA: The Project Management Institute.

Prosci, 2012. *Best Practices in Change Management*, Loveland, CO: Prosci. pp.48–51.

Knowledge Component 8.1:
Change within project governance structures

Understanding change initiatives, programmes and projects

'To form a new government requires infinite care and unbounded attention; for if the foundation is badly laid, the superstructure must be bad.'

George Washington

DEFINITION

Governance is described as ensuring 'that policies and strategy are actually implemented, and that required processes are correctly followed. Governance includes defining roles and responsibilities, measuring and reporting, and taking actions to resolve any issues identified' (Best Management Practice, 2012).

EXPLANATION

Effective change managers understand the hierarchy of projects, programmes and portfolios:

- **A project** is a specific and well defined piece of work that sits outside everyday work and is intended to change business as usual. Projects are spread across a period of time and require several people to work together who may not normally work together.

- **A programme** is used to manage a group of inter-related changes, each of which may have its own project.

- **A portfolio** is a group of proposed or current projects and programmes, which may be the whole set of changes being undertaken by an organization or a major subset of these changes.

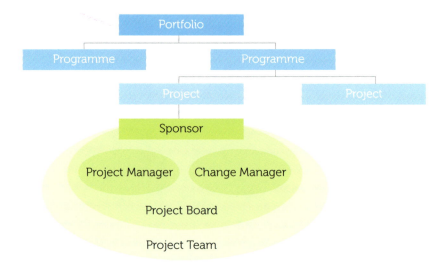

Change management may be represented at several levels within this hierarchy and effective change managers know at which level they and other change managers are working. They need to liaise with change managers and project or programme managers at each level.

It is usual for organizations to set up temporary governance structures for the management of change initiatives, even if their span reaches across several years. Some organizations might also have a Portfolio Management Office or a combined 'Portfolio, Programme and Project Office', setting standards and coordinating across the hierarchy. This is more likely to be a permanent organization structure.

The role and purpose of these structures is to ensure coordination between all the parts of the change initiative, and to understand and resolve any potential conflicts in resources and timing. Effective change managers use these structures to help identify where the cumulative impact of many changes may create risk. Change managers also know how stakeholders are represented in the portfolio, programme and project structures.

Of particular interest to effective change managers is a Change Management Office (CMO), when such a structure exists. A CMO typically provides a focal point for all organizational change initiatives. How a CMO relates to any Portfolio, Programme and Project Offices will be clearly identified.

Generally speaking, the larger the organization the more formalized these structures are. A mixture of temporary staff, contracted for part or all of the change initiative, and permanent staff seconded to the initiative may be employed during these temporary structures.

Whatever temporary or permanent structure is used, effective change managers coordinate with managers and other roles at various levels in the project hierarchy as well as with the normal everyday 'business as usual' structures.

KNOWLEDGE

The knowledge expected of an effective Change Manager is:

1. Common concepts and terms relating to project management, programme management, and portfolio management.

2. The links and dependencies between projects, programmes and portfolios, and how the change initiative relates to each of these.

3. The difference between 'waterfall' and 'agile' approaches to project management.

4. The typical project, programme, and portfolio roles (such as project managers, project sponsors, programme managers) as well as governance boards or steering committees, and how they relate to change management.

5. The role and purpose of a Change Management Office.

6. How authority and delegation typically cascades through these roles, and how reports and escalation flow up through these structures.

See also:

Knowledge Component 4.3: Managing relationships and mobilizing stakeholders

Knowledge Component 5.4: Planning communications

Knowledge Area 6: Change Impact

REFERENCES

Cabinet Office, Best Management Practice,. *Best Management Practice Portfolio: common glossary of terms and definitions*. [pdf] Available at: <http://www.best-management-practice.com/Glossaries-and-Acronyms/Common-Glossary/?DI=635845> [Accessed 11 July 2013]. Version 1.

Cabinet Office, 2011. *Managing Successful Programmes*. 4th ed. London: TSO.

Cabinet Office, 2009. *Managing Successful Projects with PRINCE2*. 5th ed. London: TSO. pp.303–314.

Cabinet Office, 2011. *Management of Portfolios*. London: TSO. pp.11–12, pp.129–133.

Cabinet Office, AXELOS, 2013. *Portfolio, Programme and Project Offices (P3O)*. London: TSO.

Change Management Learning Center,. *The Change Management Office (CMO)*. [online] Available at: <http://www.change-management.com/tutorial-who-does-cm-mod6.htm> [Accessed 29 August 2013].

DSDM Consortium, 2012. *Agile Project Management Handbook*. Version 1.1, Ashford, Kent: DSDM Consortium.

Project Management Institute, 2013. *A Guide to the Project Management Body of Knowledge (PMBOK® Guide)*. 5th ed. Newtown Square, PA: The Project Management Institute. pp.523–567.

Project Management Institute, 2013. *The Standard for Portfolio Management*. 3rd ed. Newtown Square, PA: The Project Management Institute. Section 1.2 and Glossary.

Project Management Institute, 2013. *The Standard for Program Management*. 3rd ed. Newtown Square, PA: The Project Management Institute. pp.165–167.

Knowledge Component 8.2: Establishing a project

Building the infrastructure to deliver change

'The single best payoff in terms of project success comes from having good project definition.'

Rand Corporation

DEFINITION

Establishing a project or programme is the task of creating the governance structures, reporting lines, and management processes that will enable delivery of desired outcomes. At the same time, plans, budgets and business cases are agreed and these provide direction and impetus for the project or programme.

EXPLANATION

Many critical decisions are made during the period when a project or programme is being established. Effective change managers are engaged in the decision-making to ensure the best possible outcome for the change initiative.

Effective change managers play an important role in establishing a project or programme:

- Ensuring a central role for the change management plan;

- Developing their own plans, budgets and resource requirements and defining how these are accounted for in the overall project or programme budget;

- Ensuring that the full cost of change is acknowledged in the business case, which may include costs of transitioning to the business and support costs after the project is closed; and

- Designing appropriate structures for the change teams across the whole project or programme.

Additionally, effective change managers understand the initiative's business case and the role of change management in supporting the realization of the benefits.

Often it is during this early stage of a project that requirements start to be gathered. This is of particular interest to change managers. Typically this means that project staff will engage with stakeholders to determine the requirements that the project needs to satisfy. Such engagement often takes the form of interviews or workshops. This is important to change management because it is a visible form of stakeholder engagement and can influence how stakeholders perceive the change. Eventually, these requirements become a significant input into the change impact assessment.

The output from establishing a project is a shared definition and understanding of many aspects of the project or programme. Typically this includes:

- The business case;

- The plans, budgets and resources required;

- Governance structures (including delegations and processes for reporting and escalation); and

- Processes for managing issues, risks, and document control.

All of this is usually documented. The organizational standards for these activities along with the accounting practices (such as internal charging for staff and the treatment of operational and capital expenses) strongly influence the output.

See also:

Knowledge Area 2: Defining Change

Knowledge Area 3: Managing benefits

Knowledge Area 4: Stakeholder Strategy

Knowledge Component 5.4: Planning communications

Knowledge Area 6: Change Impact

Knowledge Area 10: Facilitation

KNOWLEDGE

The knowledge expected of an effective Change Manager is:

1. The typical contents of the documentation that defines a well-established project.

2. Best practice approaches to managing issues, risks and document control.

3. Considerations in designing change team structures appropriate to the initiative and the organization.

4. Typical approaches for gathering requirements in both 'waterfall' and 'agile' styles of project development.

REFERENCES

Cabinet Office, 2011. *Managing Successful Programmes*. 4th ed. London: TSO. Chapter 4.

Cabinet Office, 2009. *Managing Successful Projects with PRINCE2*. 5th ed. London: TSO. pp.33–43, pp.263–275.

Cabinet Office, 2011. *Management of Portfolios*. London: TSO. pp.101–103.

DSDM Consortium, 2012. *Agile Project Management Handbook*. Version 1.1, Ashford, Kent: DSDM Consortium. pp.37–43.

Project Management Institute, 2013. *The Standard for Program Management*. 3rd ed. Newtown Square, PA: The Project Management Institute. p.84.

Project Management Institute, 2013. *A Guide to the Project Management Body of Knowledge (PMBOK® Guide)*. 5th ed. Newtown Square, PA: The Project Management Institute. pp.20–37.

Knowledge Component 8.3:
Change planning and scheduling

Working out what needs to be done and the resources required

'Those who plan do better than those who do not plan even though they rarely stick to their plan.'

Winston Churchill.

DEFINITION

A plan is a detailed proposal for doing or achieving something which specifies the *what, when, how* and *by whom*; and 'planning' is 'an activity responsible for creating one or more plans' (Best Management Practice, 2012). In the context of a change initiative, this means scheduling change activities and estimating budgets and other resources required.

EXPLANATION

Projects and programmes develop delivery plans that describe at different levels of detail:

- The requirements for time, budgets and resources in order to develop, review and approve the deliverables;

- A schedule of when these activities will happen; and

- The dependencies between them.

Effective change managers understand the project and programme plans, as well as developing their own schedules and budgets. They also manage the dependencies between change management work and other project work. Change management budgets and the plans for change management need to be in step with one another.

Typically there are several levels of plan, varying from detailed plans for creating a specific deliverable to high level plans across a programme of several years' duration. These plans form the baseline against which progress can be reported.

Effective change managers appreciate that planning requires consultation, negotiation and compromise. It is always inexact. They also realize that plans are a starting point, and change managers adapt to changing circumstances and replan accordingly. A well-established project or programme has an agreed procedure for modifying plans.

See also:

Knowledge Area 4:
Stakeholder Strategy

Knowledge Area 5:
Communication and
Engagement

Knowledge
Component 7.4:
Measuring change
effectiveness

Knowledge Area
9: Education and
Learning Support

KNOWLEDGE

The knowledge expected of an effective Change Manager is:

1. Common planning concepts (such as 'effort versus duration', 'critical paths', and 'Gantt charts').

2. The concepts of 'iterative development' and 'time-boxing' (an 'agile' approach) and how this affects the structure of delivery plans.

3. The typical activities that should be included in the plan for a change initiative, such as:

   • Major engagements with stakeholders;
   • Development and delivery of communications;
   • Measuring change effectiveness (for example by using surveys in scheduled events);
   • Development and delivery of training; and
   • Transitioning to the business.

4. The process of developing plans for change management including methods for identifying dependencies, budgeting for resources, and scheduling.

5. The use of common project planning software (such as Microsoft Project and Microsoft Excel).

REFERENCES

Cabinet Office, 2009. *Managing Successful Projects with PRINCE2.* 5th ed. London: TSO. pp.61–72, pp.279–283.

Project Management Institute, 2013. *A Guide to the Project Management Body of Knowledge (PMBOK® Guide).* 5th ed. Newtown Square, PA: The Project Management Institute. pp.141–192.

Knowledge Component 8.4: Executing change within a project environment

Delivering on the plans

'A good idea is about 10%, and implementation and hard work and luck is 90%.'

Guy Kawasaki, (Ex-Apple)

DEFINITION

Executing change within a project environment means delivering change management outcomes, while working with project or programme managers, using established processes, good practice, and reporting progress.

EXPLANATION

Consistent processes across the programmes and projects are normally established based on existing organizational standards and best practice. Effective change managers use these processes to help to ensure quality outcomes.

These processes include:

- Delegating work, checking the quality of the work, and monitoring and reporting progress;

- Being prepared to review and change plans and deliverables in an orderly manner;

- Proactively looking for risks and issues, managing them and escalating them where necessary;

- Monitoring and controlling the budget; and

- Engaging and managing outside suppliers.

Change managers expect to be held accountable for the quality of their deliverables, their ability to manage to a plan and a budget, and the quality of their reporting.

Information collected about change management effectiveness can also be used as the basis for progress reporting and demonstrating the effectiveness of change management. This can include 'hard' measures – such as progress with training – and 'soft' measures – such as levels of engagement. Change managers know how to use this information as part of a reporting process with varying levels of management as the target audience.

A crucial aspect of the effective execution of change is the development of an effective change team. This requires an understanding of team dynamics and of leadership.

Change is necessarily an adaptive process: people may react in unpredictable ways, and other elements of the project or programme implementation plan may be rescheduled. While executing change, effective change managers are constantly evaluating progress, looking ahead, and adjusting their approach and plans.

See also:

Knowledge Component 6.2: Assessing and managing the risks of change

Knowledge Component 7.4: Measuring change effectiveness

Knowledge Component 12.1: Leadership principles

Knowledge Component 12.2: Building team effectiveness

KNOWLEDGE

The knowledge expected of an effective Change Manager is:

1. Building and managing an effective team.

2. Effectively delegating work.

3. Good practices for:

    -   Issue management
    -   Risk management
    -   Forecasting
    -   Quality checking
    -   Monitoring of budgets and progress
    -   Progress reporting, including:
        –   Cost and progress in developing, checking and delivering change-related deliverables, and
        –   Measuring their effectiveness
    -   Scope control and configuration management
    -   Escalation, if necessary
    -   Periodical project reviews, and
    -   Vendor management (procurement).

4. How and when to change the plan for the initiative if necessary.

REFERENCES

Cabinet Office, 2009. *Managing Successful Projects with PRINCE2*. 5th ed. London: TSO. pp.99–109, pp.165–202.

DSDM Consortium, 2012. *Agile Project Management Handbook*. Version 1.1, Ashford, Kent: DSDM Consortium. pp.76–110, pp.117–123.

Project Management Institute, 2013. *A Guide to the Project Management Body of Knowledge (PMBOK® Guide)*. 5th ed. Newtown Square, PA: The Project Management Institute. pp.79–100.

Knowledge Component 8.5: Transitioning to the business

Handing back to the organization

'Innumerable confusions and a feeling of despair invariably emerge in periods of great technological and cultural transition.'

Marshall McLuhan

DEFINITION

In the context of a change initiative, transitioning to the business is handing over deliverables to 'business as usual' in such a way that the appropriate people at all levels in the organization feel ready, willing and able to take ownership, leading to sustainable benefits.

EXPLANATION

Activities in transitioning to the business vary widely according to the nature of the change initiative but often include:

- Reviewing, checking and testing deliverables;

- Training and education in the use and support of the deliverables;

- Periods of pilot trials and parallel running;

- Final cut-over to new systems, new processes, new ways of working and a formal handover of ownership;

- Closing down of replaced assets (for example buildings or systems), which can be an emotional time for some stakeholders; and

- A review of what was achieved and what was not, including lessons that can be passed on.

Project managers lead many of these activities. However, they require considerable engagement and effort from key stakeholder groups. Effective change managers are closely involved in planning, implementing and monitoring these activities. Although these activities are discussed during planning, ideas commonly evolve as the change initiative proceeds.

Transition is a time where 'taking the temperature' is especially important and reactions can change quite dramatically in a short time. The techniques explained in *Measuring change effectiveness* (Knowledge Component 7.4) are just as important in this period as at any time in the change initiative.

Effective change managers pay particular attention to stakeholder reactions during the transition period, especially where the deliverables are failing to meet expectations or where the training is proving to be ineffective.

Careful consideration is given to the risks of deliverables failing to deliver intended outcomes. Ways of mitigating these risks include pilot trials, gradual implementation (as opposed to a single, all-or-nothing cut-over) and periods of parallel running. All these may lead to extra work for stakeholders. Gradual implementation may be centrally planned, or may offer stakeholders the choice of 'signing up' for early or late implementation. Choice of the appropriate approach often requires expertise from project management, technical and change management specialists.

In a project that is using a more iterative approach (including 'agile' project development) transition points to the business can occur throughout the project.

See also:

Knowledge Area 3: Managing Benefits

Knowledge Area 4: Stakeholder Strategy

Knowledge Component 6.2: Assessing and managing the risks of change

Knowledge Component 6.3: Business continuity and contingency during change

Knowledge Component 7.4: Measuring change effectiveness

Knowledge Area 9: Education and Learning Support

KNOWLEDGE

The knowledge expected of an effective Change Manager is:

1. The advantages and disadvantages of different approaches to transition, including:

   - Pilot trials;
   - Parallel running; and
   - Gradual implementation.

2. Key questions from a change management perspective during the transition period, such as:

   - How effective has training been and what needs to be done to address any gaps?
   - What is the gap between stakeholder expectations and the reality of the deliverables?
   - Is ongoing support available?
   - Is the business ready to adopt and sustain the change?
   - Are new behaviours and attitudes being demonstrated as expected?
   - What further changes need to be made to enable the business to deliver the benefits?
   - What lessons were learned for the next part of the change initiative?

REFERENCES

Cabinet Office, 2009. *Managing Successful Projects with PRINCE2*. 5th ed. London: TSO. pp.99–109, pp.165–202.

DSDM Consortium, 2012. *Agile Project Management Handbook*. Version 1.1, Ashford, Kent: DSDM Consortium. pp.76–110, pp.117–123.

Project Management Institute, 2013. *A Guide to the Project Management Body of Knowledge (PMBOK® Guide)*. 5th ed. Newtown Square, PA: The Project Management Institute. pp.79–100.

Knowledge Area 9: Education and Learning Support
Training and supporting change

BACKGROUND

Every change has consequences for individuals, and requires people to change and develop their repertoire of behaviours. People need to learn new information (knowledge), new skills and new attitudes. They may also have to 'unlearn' patterns of behaviour that have been established over many years.

From a change management perspective, this means that an understanding of how adults learn and develop offers important insights into the change process. From a practical point of view, a change management plan includes training and coaching elements to help people to learn how they can work effectively within the changed environment. In many cases the primary work of identifying learning needs and developing plans to meet those needs is the responsibility of a specialist Learning and Development (L&D) or Human Resources Development (HRD) function. However effective change managers contribute to developing and critiquing such plans, ensuring that they align with the wider change initiative.

On occasions change managers need to act as trainers, either in change management topics – to pass on knowledge and understanding of their own discipline – or on technical training, as their personal skill set allows. This, too, requires effective change managers to understand good training and learning practices.

Coaching is a specific technique which supports learning, and which may have a place in change initiatives. Specialist resources are often available to help to construct wider coaching plans. However, effective change managers need to coach colleagues through the change initiative. As a result, an understanding of basic coaching theory is a valuable part of their skill set.

It is not expected that change managers will have the depth of knowledge or skill in these areas that would be required of Learning and Development (L&D) or Human Resources Development (HRD) professionals. However, they should be sufficiently knowledgeable to make effective use of such expertise and to offer helpful direction to line management in the absence of such professional support.

KNOWLEDGE COMPONENTS

These Knowledge Components are essential to training and support during change:

1. Learning theory and skills development

2. Identifying and meeting learning needs

3. Behavioural change and coaching

EDUCATION AND LEARNING SUPPORT IN PRACTICE

Effective change managers understand how adults learn and develop. This offers them important insights into the change process and into how change impacts on performance. They work with specialists in Learning and Development (L&D) or Human Resources (HR) to ensure the learning needs of individuals and teams affected by change are integral to the change management plan. The resulting training plan takes account of individual learning styles and preferences. This leads to effective design of instructional sessions that deliver the knowledge, skills and attitudes required by the change initiative. While change managers occasionally present training, they usually give valued support to colleagues in designing their own sessions, or connect them with specialist resources to advise them on a range of blended learning options.

From time to time senior leaders seek out the change manager for personal advice and support on challenges they face in designing, implementing or embedding change initiatives.

Where the required behavioural changes are not susceptible to training, change managers provide effective coaching (including processes for feedback and active listening) to line managers to enable them to plan to coach others.

HOW THIS KNOWLEDGE AREA SUPPORTS
THE CMI CHANGE MANAGEMENT PRACTITIONER COMPETENCIES

Related Change Manager Practitioner Competencies	9.1 Learning theory and skills development	9.2 Identifying and meeting learning needs	9.3 Behavioural change and coaching
Facilitating Change			O
Strategic Thinking			O
Coaching for Change	O	O	O
Specialist Expertise – Learning & Development	O	O	O

KEY REFERENCES FOR THIS KNOWLEDGE AREA

Cameron, E. and Green, M., 2012. *Making Sense of Change Management: a complete guide to the models, tools and techniques of organizational change.* 3rd ed. London: Kogan Page.

Harrison, R., 2009. Learning and Development. 5th ed. London: Chartered Institute of Personnel and Development.

Huczynski, A.A. and Buchanan, D.A., 2007. *Organizational Behaviour.* 6th ed. Harlow, Essex: Pearson Education.

Knowledge Component 9.1:
Learning Theory and Skills Development

Stimulating effective learning and development

'We now accept the fact that learning is a lifelong process of keeping abreast of change. And the most pressing task is to teach people how to learn.'
Peter Drucker

DEFINITION

Learning is described as 'the process of acquiring knowledge through experience which leads to an enduring change in behaviour' (Huczynski and Buchanan, 2007). However others have offered wider ideas about learning. It is 'a qualitative change in a person's way of seeing, experiencing, understanding, conceptualising something in the real world' (Marton and Ramsden, 1988). Learning includes both the procedural elements required to complete a task and gaining the underpinning or background understanding and attitudes needed to perform the task effectively in its organizational context.

EXPLANATION

Effective change managers understand the key principles of adult learning, including motivation to learn and the learning process. This is needed because at an individual level, learning is an integral part of the change process. As a result, all change initiatives must take account of the 'enduring changes in behaviour' required of people affected. It is essential that the related training builds confidence as well as competence.

Change managers who understand how people learn are better able to plan. They can allocate realistic time and resources to achieve desired behaviour change. They can also better predict the impact on performance which will result from the learning process people will undergo.

See also:

Knowledge Component 7.1: Building individual motivation to change

Knowledge Component 11.3: Reinforcement systems

Knowledge Component 12.1: Leadership principles

KNOWLEDGE

The knowledge expected of an effective Change Manager is:

1. Key aspects of motivation to learn and how this can be enhanced, including both general motivation theory and the specific factors affecting learning during change (fear of consequences resulting from failure to change or from failure in the learning process).

2. The relationship between the learning process and job performance.

3. The process of experiential learning in adults, and how learning designs which pay appropriate attention to the 'learning cycle' help to ensure proper development of skills and knowledge.

4. How to address learning to people with different:

    *   Learning preferences (Honey and Mumford, 1982); and
    *   Preferred ways of receiving information – for example visual, auditory, reading or kinaesthetic (Pashler et al., 2009).

5. The impact of different learning methods on retention of learning.

REFERENCES

Cameron, E. and Green, M., 2012. *Making Sense of Change Management: a complete guide to the models, tools and techniques of organizational change.* 3rd ed. London: Kogan Page. pp.16–35.

Harrison, R., 2009. *Learning and Development.* 5th ed. London: Chartered Institute of Personnel and Development.

Honey, P. and Mumford, A., 1982. *Manual of Learning Styles.* Oxford, Oxfordshire: Peter Honey Publications.

Huczynski, A.A. and Buchanan, D.A., 2007. *Organizational Behaviour.* 6th ed. Harlow, Essex: Pearson Education. pp.103–135.

Marton, F. and Ramsden, P., 1988. What does it take to improve learning? In: Ramsden, P. (ed.) *Improving Learning: New Perspectives.* London: Kogan Page. p.271 (Cited in Harrison 2009, p.95)

Pashler, H., McDaniel, M., Rohrer, D. and Bjork, R., 2009. Learning styles: concepts and evidence. *Psychological Science in the Public Interest,* 9(3), pp.105–119.

Knowledge Component 9.2:
Identifying and meeting learning needs

Assessing learning needs, developing training plans and evaluating outcomes

'Tell me and I forget. Teach me and I remember. Involve me and I learn.'

Benjamin Franklin

DEFINITION

Meeting learning needs during a change initiative is the end-to-end process, integrated with the initiative, of ensuring that the skills, knowledge and attitudes of those affected by the change are developed in a way that supports successful change.

EXPLANATION

Effective change managers understand the need to ensure that the behaviours of those affected by a change are aligned with the desired 'end state' of a change process. They make appropriate use of information already available in the organization to define a skills baseline and to draw on a range of techniques to:

- Identify the learning needs that a change generates;

- Construct a learning and development plan;

- Source appropriate training or other development activity;

- Evaluate the effectiveness of training; and

- Ensure its effective application in the workplace.

Effective change managers ensure that plans for various aspects of their change initiatives take account of the timing with which new skills will be required. The plans they formulate include sufficient time and resources for the Learning and Development (L&D) activity that is needed, and align with other activities which may be impacting those who need to learn. They use professional support from L&D or Human Resources Development (HRD) practitioners wherever available.

The effective change manager's knowledge in this area should be sufficient to construct workable training plans in the absence of specialist Learning and Development support.

KNOWLEDGE

The knowledge expected of an effective Change Manager is:

1. The principles of analysing learning or training needs, including sources of information in the organization about skills and competence.

2. Methods of analysing a job into the knowledge, skills and attitudes required.

3. How to develop an appropriate training plan, which:

   - Takes full account of both learning needs and the logistics of providing training; and
   - Aligns with other aspects of the change management plan.

4. Considerations in planning effective instructional sessions to train skills and to communicate knowledge, including principles of good instructional design.

5. The advantages and disadvantages of different learning channels (including when and how to use different approaches), such as:

   - Classroom;
   - The facilitated virtual classroom; and
   - Other forms of e-learning.

6. Principles of evaluating training effectiveness, including different levels of, and purposes for, evaluation.

REFERENCES

Chartered Institute of Personnel and Development (CIPD), 2013. *Identifying Learning and Talent Development Needs.* [online] Available at: <http://www.cipd.co.uk/hr-resources/factsheets/identifying-learning-talent-development-needs.aspx> [Accessed 25 July 2013].

Gagne, R.M., Wager, W.W., Golas, K.C. and Keller, J.M., 2004. *Principles of Instructional Design.* 5th ed. Belmont, CA: Wadsworth.

Harrison, R., 2009. *Learning and Development.* 5th ed. London: Chartered Institute of Personnel and Development. Chapters 7 and 15.

Huczynski, A.A. and Buchanan, D.A., 2007. *Organizational Behaviour.* 6th ed. Harlow, Essex: Pearson Education. pp.103–135.

Kirkpatrick, D.L. and Kirkpatrick, J.D., 2006. *Evaluating Training Programs: the four levels.* San Francisco, CA: Berrett-Koehler.

See also:

Knowledge Component 7.1: Building individual motivation to change

Knowledge Component 11.3: Reinforcement systems

Knowledge Component 12.1: Leadership principles

Knowledge Component 9.3:
Behavioural Change and coaching

Supporting people through feedback and coaching

'You cannot teach a man anything. You can only help him discover it within himself.'

Galileo Galilei

DEFINITION

Behavioural change is the process through which people adjust the way they characteristically operate in the world. It includes the underlying patterns that others might see as their personal 'style', and which critically affects the responses people make to them. There are various definitions of coaching, but here we define coaching in the workplace as 'the continuous process of developing an individual's performance by using work situations (day-to-day or specially arranged) to provide planned learning opportunities supported by agreed guidance and feedback' (Smith, 2000).

EXPLANATION

Some behaviours are not susceptible to 'training' but they can be developed – given the right context and encouragement. This is particularly true of a range of interpersonal behaviours and styles. Effective change managers understand how the key principles of adult learning apply to these behaviours and how people can be helped through the process of developing them. Specifically they understand the processes of feedback and coaching to a sufficient depth to provide effective coaching to line management colleagues, and to help them plan to coach subordinates. A change manager is not expected to have the level of expertise required to develop coaching skills in others.

KNOWLEDGE

The knowledge expected of an effective Change Manager is:

1. Principles and practices of:

   • Giving effective developmental feedback; and
   • Active listening.

2. A well-respected coaching framework, which can serve as a process template for a coaching interaction and for an overall coaching process, and includes the elements of:

   • Contracting;
   • Goal-setting;
   • Exploration of development options and opportunities;
   • Conditions for feedback; and
   • Closure of the coaching process.

See also:

Knowledge Component 5.1: Theory of effective communicating

Knowledge Component 7.1: Building individual motivation to change

REFERENCES

APMG-International, 2013. *Change Management Practitioner Handbook*. Version 1.5. High Wycombe, Buckinghamshire: APMG-International. Section 1.

Cameron, E. and Green, M., 2012. *Making Sense of Change Management: a complete guide to the models, tools and techniques of organizational change*. 3rd ed. London: Kogan Page. pp.28–35.

Chartered Institute of Personnel and Development (CIPD), 2012. *Coaching and Mentoring*. [online] Available at: <https://www.cipd.co.uk/hr-resources/factsheets/coaching-mentoring.aspx> [Accessed 25 July 2013].

Harrison, R., 2009. *Learning and Development*. 5th ed. London: Chartered Institute of Personnel and Development. pp.167–171.

Huczynski, A.A. and Buchanan, D.A., 2007. *Organizational Behaviour*. 6th ed. Harlow, Essex: Pearson Education. pp.103–135.

Smith, I.R., 2000. *Coaching Notes*. Unpublished

Whitmore, J., 2009. *Coaching for Performance: GROWing Human Potential and Purpose*. 4th ed. London: Nicholas Brealey.

Knowledge Area 10: Facilitation

Facilitating group events through a change

BACKGROUND

Group facilitation is the act of planning and managing a process that will enable a group of people in a meeting or workshop to reach a set of objectives. Facilitators manage the process of reaching the objectives, but do not influence the shape and content of the objectives. In other words, a facilitator guides a group towards a destination and makes it easier for them to get there. Good facilitation builds ownership of the outcomes and, because of this, is a useful tool for engaging with stakeholders and assuring robust results.

Effective group facilitation is a valuable tool for all types of managers – effective change managers are also effective facilitators. The change management process often demands a large number of well-facilitated events. These enable individuals and groups to participate and work together, improving collaboration and shared learning. There are many uses for group facilitation, including these ones that are directly relevant to change management:

- Identifying issues, risks or stakeholders;

- Communicating to, engaging with and gaining feedback from stakeholders to build awareness of the change;

- Defining the change and developing a vision;

- Finding solutions to actual or potential problems;

- Developing strategy; and

- Planning communications and training.

Increasingly, there is a virtual element to many meetings and workshops and effective change managers are prepared for this.

KNOWLEDGE COMPONENTS

These Knowledge Components are essential to successful facilitation:

- The role of the facilitator and the skills required

- Preparing a group process

- Facilitating a group process

FACILITATION IN PRACTICE

An effective change manager facilitates many workshops through the life of a change initiative. Each workshop has a clear set of objectives and relevant participants are identified. The style and approach of the workshop is chosen and combined with the objectives to design an agenda that fits the time available, will achieve the objectives, and gives all participants an opportunity to contribute and take ownership of the results. There are many approaches to facilitation and many techniques for collaborative work. These are selected as being appropriate to the task, suitable for the participants, and compatible with the prevailing culture of the participants.

An effective change manager remains observant throughout the workshop, adapting the approach as the need arises. The last part of the agenda includes a review of the workshop, what it achieved, and any outstanding actions. When participants leave a workshop with a sense of achievement, it has made a valuable contribution to engagement and progress with the change initiative.

HOW THIS KNOWLEDGE AREA SUPPORTS
THE CMI CHANGE MANAGEMENT PRACTITIONER COMPETENCIES

Related Change Manager Practitioner Competencies	10.1 The role of the facilitator and the skills required	10.2 Preparing a group process	10.3 Facilitating a group process
Influencing Others	O		
Coaching for Change	O	O	O
Communication Skills	O	O	O
Facilitation	O	O	O
Specialist Expertise – Learning & Development	O	O	O
Specialist Expertise – Communication	O	O	O

KEY REFERENCES FOR THIS KNOWLEDGE AREA

From the many useful introductions and guides about facilitation that are available online we recommend:

International Association of Facilitators, 2002. *Basic Facilitation Skills.* [pdf] Available at: <http://www.iaf-world.org/Libraries/Facilitation_Articles/ASQ-IAF_Facilitation_Primer.sflb.ashx> [Accessed 23 July 2013].

Keating, C., 2003. *Facilitation Toolkit: a practical guide to working more effectively with people and groups.* [pdf] (Department of Environmental Protection, Water and Rivers Commission; Department of Conservation and Land Management (Western Australia)) Available at: <http://portal.environment.wa.gov.au/pls/portal/docs/PAGE/DOE_ADMIN/PUBLICATION_REPOSITORY/FACILITATION%20TOOLKIT.PDF> [Accessed 23 July 2013].

Also useful:

Interaction Associates, 2007. *20 Simple Ways to Improve Virtual Meetings.* [pdf] Available at: <http://www.interactionassociates.com/pdf/IA_20_Simple_Ways_To_Improve_Virtual_Meetings.pdf> [Accessed 23 July 2013].

A good list of techniques and tools can be found in:

Mann, T., 2012. *Facilitation: a manual of models, tools and techniques for effective group working.* Newbury, Berkshire: Resource Publications.

More in-depth resources for the experienced facilitator who wants to learn include:

Schwarz, R., Davidson, A., Carlson, P. and McKinney, S., 2005. *The Skilled Facilitator Fieldbook: tips, tools, and tested methods for consultants, facilitators, managers, trainers, and coaches.* San Francisco, CA: Jossey-Bass.

Schuman, S., 2007. *The IAF Handbook of Group Facilitation: best practices from the leading organization in facilitation.* San Francisco, CA: Jossey-Bass.

Knowledge Component 10.1:
The role of the facilitator

Helping people to work together and achieve their objectives

'The facilitator impacts and guides the process but does not give input on the content of a meeting – that comes from the participants.'
Kelsey, D., & Plumb, P

DEFINITION

A facilitator is an individual who develops and manages the processes and structure for a workshop or meeting so that it can be effective in achieving its objectives. The facilitator focuses on the agenda, processes and dynamics of the meeting, thereby allowing the participants to focus on the core subject matter and work together effectively.

EXPLANATION

Effective change managers know that good facilitation requires clear objectives and strong preparation. The preparation takes into account the nature and complexity of the objectives, together with consideration of the number and nature of the participants.

Effective change managers select facilitation styles, approaches and techniques that allow achievement of the objectives, acting in such a way that the participants take ownership of the end results. However, effective facilitators know that approaches and agendas need to remain flexible. If the need arises they know when and how to adjust the agenda during the workshop.

Good facilitation starts at the opening of the workshop, where the facilitator will establish a positive tone and agree objectives and ground rules. During the workshop, the facilitator needs to observe the group dynamics and individual reactions, always prepared to intervene to keep the group focussed and ensure that all viewpoints are being considered.

An effective facilitator is practised, confident, able to listen and question well, self-aware, respectful, open, honest, flexible and observant.

KNOWLEDGE

The knowledge expected of an effective Change Manager is:

1. Understanding of personality types and how they react in group settings.

2. Techniques of questioning and active listening.

3. How technology can be used during both physical and virtual meetings.

4. A variety of techniques that enable groups to:

   - Identify known information;
   - Create new ideas;
   - Encourage conversations that engage and create;
   - Plan;
   - Prioritise, connecting and comparing ideas;
   - Problem-solve;
   - Reach consensus or articulate differences;
   - Learn together; and
   - Work in large scale workshops.

5. Techniques for capturing and organizing the information generated in a session.

REFERENCES

From the many useful introductions and guides to facilitation that are available online, one especially helpful publication is:

Keating, C., 2003. *Facilitation Toolkit: a practical guide to working more effectively with people and groups*. [pdf] (Department of Environmental Protection, Water and Rivers Commission; Department of Conservation and Land Management (Western Australia)) Available at: <http://portal.environment. wa.gov.au/pls/portal/docs/PAGE/DOE_ADMIN/PUBLICATION_REPOSITORY/ FACILITATION%20TOOLKIT.PDF> [Accessed 7 October 2013].

Also useful:

International Association of Facilitators, 2003. *Basic IAF Core Competencies for Certification*. [online] Available at: <http://www.iaf-world.org/index/ certification/CompetenciesforCertification.aspx> [Accessed 18 September 2013].

Interaction Associates, 2007. *20 Simple Ways to Improve Virtual Meetings*. [pdf] Available at: <http://www.interactionassociates.com/pdf/IA_20_Simple_ Ways_To_Improve_Virtual_Meetings.pdf> [Accessed 23 July 2013].

A good list of techniques and tools can be found in:

Mann, T., 2012. *Facilitation: a manual of models, tools and techniques for effective group working*. Newbury, Berkshire: Resource Publications.

See also:

Knowledge Component 1.2: Change and the individual

Knowledge Component 9.1: Learning theory and skills development

Knowledge Component 12.2: Building team effectiveness

Knowledge Component 12.3: Emotional intelligence

Knowledge Component 10.2:
Preparing a group process

Effective planning and preparation for successful events

'Before anything else, preparation is the key to success.'
Alexander Graham Bell

DEFINITION

The process of designing a facilitated group event on a solid foundation of understanding the objectives, the constraints and the participants.

EXPLANATION

Any facilitated process involving people is an important event in a change initiative. Participants invest their personal time, energy and commitment, and the facilitator has an obligation to set and manage their expectations appropriately. Effective change managers know that successful events are built on a solid foundation of effective planning and preparation, so they consider these factors when planning an event:

- Purpose – why is the event needed and what are the objectives?

- Product – what output is required?

- Participants – who is involved and what are their perspectives?

- Probable issues – what concerns will arise and are there any obstacles that could prevent success?

- Process – what are the steps and timeframes required, and how might they change as the event proceeds?

- Place – what is an appropriate venue for the event?

- Practical tools – what materials and technologies are required?

This often requires several conversations with the person or people who are proposing the workshop. It may also be necessary to negotiate the scope of the objectives and the time allowed.

KNOWLEDGE

The knowledge expected of an effective Change Manager is:

See also:

Knowledge
Component 12.5:
Negotiation

1. The advantages and disadvantages of using independent facilitators who are not usually associated with the participants.

2. Different facilitation activities:

   - How they contribute to objectives;
   - How they allow people with different working styles to collaborate and learn together;
   - How the activities can be combined to create an agenda that leads to:
     – Achieving the objectives in the given time and
     – The participants' feeling of ownership; and
   - How the output from each activity can be recorded.

3. Types of technology and materials required for the support of the agenda.

4. Approaches for selecting participants to attend the session and how they can be prepared in an optimal way.

5. The main criteria for deciding what support will be required to capture and record information and manage technology.

6. The factors and considerations relevant to choosing and preparing the venue, the room layout and adjusting these if needed as the event progresses.

REFERENCES

International Association of Facilitators, 2002. *Basic Facilitation Skills*. [pdf] Available at: <http://www.iaf-world.org/Libraries/Facilitation_Articles/ASQ-IAF_Facilitation_Primer.sflb.ashx> [Accessed 23 July 2013]. pp.10–14.

Keating, C., 2003. *Facilitation Toolkit: A practical guide to working more effectively with people and groups*. [pdf] (Department of Environmental Protection, Water and Rivers Commission; Department of Conservation and Land Management (Western Australia)) Available at: <http://portal.environment.wa.gov.au/pls/portal/docs/PAGE/DOE_ADMIN/PUBLICATION_REPOSITORY/FACILITATION%20TOOLKIT.PDF> [Accessed 23 July 2013]. Section B, Section D and Appendix IV.

Mittleman, D.D., Briggs, R.O. and Nunamaker, J.F., 2000. Best Practices in Facilitating Virtual Meetings: some notes from initial experiences. *Group Facilitation: A Research and Applications Journal*, Winter Issue.

Knowledge Component 10.3: Facilitating a group process

Guiding the process, adapting, and managing the ebb and flow

'Group facilitation is a process in which a person whose selection is acceptable to all the members of the group, who is substantively neutral, and who has no substantive decision-making authority diagnoses and intervenes to help a group improve how it identifies and solves problems and makes decisions, to increase the group's effectiveness.'

R. Schwarz, 2002.

DEFINITION

Facilitating a group is managing the process to help the group to reach the best possible result and take ownership of it.

EXPLANATION

As effective facilitators, change managers approach a facilitation session with a methodically prepared plan, or agenda, and with an understanding of who the stakeholders are. However, no plan is perfect, and in a change initiative, such sessions are often key to successful stakeholder engagement. Because the objectives of an event are important and matter to the participants, feelings and emotions may run high. The effective facilitator is able to guide the process, adapt the plan when necessary and manage the ebb and flow of behaviours and feelings in the meeting.

Group facilitation is about working with people and assisting them in their interactions. This means that it is important to understand the differences in how people think, learn and operate.

Effective change managers establish a positive and participative atmosphere from the beginning of an event. Then, during the event, they constantly evaluate the agenda and know when and how to modify it. They are looking for any signs showing that:

- The objectives are more complex than originally thought

- People are either withdrawing or dominating, or

- The planned activities are failing to achieve results.

As effective facilitators, change managers recognize the need to intervene, and choose an appropriate style and method of intervention. This is easier if ground rules have been negotiated with the group *at the beginning* of a session or series of sessions.

Group closure offers an opportunity to check that objectives have been achieved, confirm outstanding work, learn from the experience and check for unresolved conflict.

Finally, follow-up after the session is important and sends the message to participants that their time and input has been valued. While change managers are not always responsible for actioning the results of a session, they ensure that follow up actions are communicated to the participants.

KNOWLEDGE

The knowledge expected of an effective Change Manager is:

1. Techniques for opening a session, setting the right tone, and establishing ground rules.

2. Interpretation of the group dynamics as they unfold.

3. Knowing whether, when and how to intervene in the process, especially to:

   • Encourage full participation;
   • Manage 'groupthink', negative emotions, and personal comments;
   • Revise the plan for the session;
   • Maintain momentum and engagement; and
   • Accommodate people who prefer to work in different ways.

4. How to work with attendees to review a facilitated session, especially:

   • What has been achieved;
   • What remains to be done; and
   • What could have been done differently.

See also:

Knowledge Component 1.2: Change and the individual

Knowledge Component 9.1: Learning theory and skills development

Knowledge Component 12.6: Conflict Management

REFERENCES

International Association of Facilitators, 2002. *Basic Facilitation Skills.* [pdf] Available at: <http://www.iaf-world.org/Libraries/Facilitation_Articles/ASQ-IAF_Facilitation_Primer.sflb.ashx> [Accessed 23 July 2013]. pp.15–28.

Keating, C., 2003. *Facilitation Toolkit: A practical guide to working more effectively with people and groups.* [pdf] (Department of Environmental Protection, Water and Rivers Commission; Department of Conservation and Land Management (Western Australia)) Available at: <http://portal.environment.wa.gov.au/pls/portal/docs/PAGE/DOE_ADMIN/PUBLICATION_REPOSITORY/FACILITATION%20TOOLKIT.PDF> [Accessed 23 July 2013]. Appendix II and Appendix III.

Mittleman, D.D., Briggs, R.O. and Nunamaker, J.F., 2000. Best Practices in Facilitating Virtual Meetings: some notes from initial experiences. *Group Facilitation: A Research and Applications Journal*, Winter Issue.

Knowledge Area 11: Sustaining Systems

How to ensure that change is sustained

BACKGROUND

For change to 'stick' new behaviours need to become an intrinsic part of the formal and informal systems, the practices and habits that form the organization's normal mode of operation. Sustaining systems are the mechanisms for achieving this; they help to reinforce the change across the organization. If this aspect of change is neglected, people can easily slide back into familiar comfort zones, and the organization could fail to see any transformation or benefit.

Sustaining systems need to be designed, planned and implemented as part of the change initiative. The range of levers deployed to ensure change is sustained must be appropriate for both the nature of the change required and the wider context within which it occurs. Some key elements that contribute to sustainable change involve:

- Showing how the change is working and why the old ways will no longer be as useful;
- Using appropriate reporting mechanisms to measure and support the sustained performance;
- Ensuring that leaders support and model the new behaviours;
- Demonstrating how changed behaviours link directly to performance improvements;
- Ensuring that reinforcement systems are in place to encourage new behaviours; and
- Removing access to former systems or other options, if appropriate.

For organizational change to be successful, there needs to be continued monitoring and evaluating of progress, so that the sustaining systems remain effective. This should cover both the process (or system elements) and the people aspects.

KNOWLEDGE COMPONENTS

The following knowledge components are essential to ensuring change is sustained:

1. Organization development levers
2. Leadership levers
3. Reinforcement systems
4. Achieving critical mass
5. Embedding change

SUSTAINING SYSTEMS IN PRACTICE

Effective change managers are concerned with ensuring people are prepared to change and can follow through – doing things differently once the change has been implemented. To achieve this they ensure the preparations and plans for change include factors such as training and organizational restructuring if required. This may also include redefining peoples' roles, the way performance is measured or new reward and incentive schemes. In this case organization development specialists are often involved in the process.

Effective change managers engage with other leaders and line managers across the organization to ensure the people they manage get the required support for adopting change. Some people may need additional coaching and feedback while they become familiar with the new ways of working.

Two important areas of focus for change managers are tracking the level of acceptance and measuring the outcomes from change. These include tracking the impact of the change initiative on the organization, from both a task and people perspective. Having effective feedback channels and monitoring systems in place means that change managers can identify and address issues early, which helps ensure that the changes become embedded and a normal part of day-to-day operations.

Related Change Manager Practitioner Competencies	11.1 Organization development levers	11.2 Leadership levers	11.3 Reinforcement systems	11.4 Achieving critical mass	11.5 Embedding change
Facilitating Change	O	O	O		O
Strategic Thinking	O	O	O		O
Thinking & Judgement	O				O
Influencing Others	O	O	O	O	O
Coaching for Change	O	O			O
Communication Skills		O		O	O
Specialist Expertise – Learning & Development	O			O	O
Specialist expertise – Communication	O			O	O

KEY REFERENCES FOR THIS KNOWLEDGE AREA

Cameron, E. and Green, M., 2012. *Making Sense of Change Management: a complete guide to the models, tools and techniques of organizational change.* 3rd ed. London: Kogan Page.

Roberto, M.A. and Levesque, L.C., 2005. The Art of Making Change Initiatives Stick. *MIT Sloan Management Review*, 46(4), SMR178, reprint no. 46410 [online] Available at: <http://www.sloanreview.mit.edu> [Accessed 26 July 2013].

Knowledge Component 11.1:
Organization development levers

Understanding the value of organization development approaches

'An organization's ability to learn, and translate that learning into action rapidly, is the ultimate competitive advantage.'

Jack Welch

DEFINITION

Organization development levers are ways in which the classic tools of the Organization Development discipline can be used to most effect in driving and embedding change.

EXPLANATION

Effective change managers recognize the importance of having appropriate organization development interventions in place to ensure changes become embedded and can be sustained. These can occur at all levels of the organization. They may involve redefining job roles, changing the way people's performance is monitored and evaluated, and how rewards and career advancement are decided. In turn, these may lead to new strategic key performance indicators and metrics.

People are more likely to accept the interventions, and find them easier to work with, if they can see clear connections with the overall aims of the change initiative. Effective change managers ensure there are appropriate measures and reporting mechanisms in place to monitor and demonstrate the impact of organization development levers on the change initiative. There must also be transparency in the way decisions are made to ensure procedural fairness.

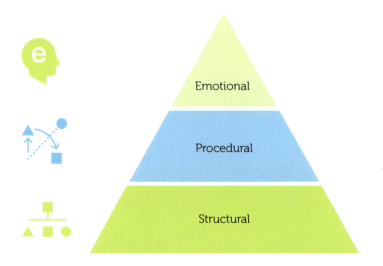

Change managers work closely with organization development specialists to design the most appropriate interventions to bring about sustainable change that will support the overarching organizational goals. An important aspect of this is to help the organization develop its change capability and capacity. A more holistic, longer-term perspective is required when designing and implementing organization development levers.

KNOWLEDGE

The knowledge expected of an effective Change Manager is:

1. Understanding a range of organization development interventions.
2. Designing effective interventions (which help to adopt change), including ones that are:
   - Structural (for example new organizational structures, monitoring and control systems, and processes and reinforcement mechanisms);
   - Procedural fairness and legitimacy; and
   - Emotional (for example handling people's anxieties and providing appropriate support structures).
3. 'Systems thinking' approaches.
4. Principles of organization development and of different organizational forms, models and structures.

See also:

Knowledge Component 7.2 Building organizational readiness for change

Knowledge Component 9.2: Indentifying and meeting learning needs

Knowledge Component 9.3: Behavioural change and coaching

Knowledge Component: 13.1: The Change Manager and Human Resources

REFERENCES

Cameron, E. and Green, M., 2012. *Making Sense of Change Management: a complete guide to the models, tools and techniques of organizational change*. 3rd ed. London: Kogan Page.

Cannon, J.A. and McGee, R., 2008. *Organisational Development and Change: CIPD toolkit*. London: CIPD.

Chapman, J.A., 2002. A Framework For Transformational Change in Organizations. *Leadership & Organization Development Journal*, 23(1), pp.16–25 [online] Available at <http://www.emeraldinsight.com/0143-7739.htm> [Accessed 24 July 2013].

Cummings, T.G. and Worley, C.G., 2009. *Organization Development and Change*. 9th ed. Mason, OH: South-Western Publishing.

Harshak, A., Aguirre, D. and Brown, A., 2010. *Making Change Happen, and Making It Stick*. [pdf] (Booz & Company Inc) Available at: <http://www.strategy-business.com/article/00057?pg=all > [Accessed 26 July 2013].

Kotter, J.P., 2012. *Leading Change*. 2nd ed. Boston, MA: Harvard Business Review Press.

Roberto, M.A. and Levesque, L.C., 2005. The Art of Making Change Initiatives Stick. *MIT Sloan Management Review*, 46(4), SMR178, reprint no. 46410 [online] Available at: <http://www.sloanreview.mit.edu> [Accessed 26 July 2013].

Senge, P.M., 1993. *The Fifth Discipline: the art and practice of the learning organization*. London: Century.

Knowledge Component 11.2:
Leadership levers

Effective leadership to embed and sustain change

'The achievements of an organization are the results of the combined effort of each individual.'

Vince Lombardi.

DEFINITION

Leadership levers that sustain change are normal leadership and management processes, applied by line managers to develop and reinforce team behaviours that are aligned with the intended change.

EXPLANATION

New ways of behaving and doing things will initially feel uncomfortable and there is a natural tendency for people to revert to their comfort zones and keep doing what they have always done. Change initiatives that last require a shift in people's attitudes as well as behaviours. Careful consideration must be given to how people's attitudes and beliefs need to change to align with the new ways of working, and the additional support this will require.

Effective change managers model good leadership, and help line managers to understand what is required of them to ensure that the change becomes embedded within the organization. Line managers need to be observant to pick up on behaviours that are not helpful and to listen out for clues about people's attitude to the change. Leadership levers contribute to:

- Creating a supportive and enabling environment to help individuals to move from awareness to acceptance of the change;

- Providing appropriate training, mentoring, support and encouragement to help to develop people's confidence in embracing change; and

- Empowering people to take responsibility for adopting the changes.

If people are not accepting of the change, line managers must diagnose the symptoms and assess at what level to address the problem, which could be a cultural or leadership issue. Leaders must be self-aware and recognize they themselves are not immune to emotional responses to change, while at the same time having to support others through this change.

Effective change managers and line managers plan for demonstrating short-term wins and use every opportunity to reinforce the links between the new behaviours and improved results.

KNOWLEDGE

The knowledge expected of an effective Change Manager is:

1. The nature of effective line management and leadership, and the levers available to those in line positions to help to embed change.

2. Recognizing symptoms of competence issues, confidence issues or lack of belief in the value of changes.

3. Models of transformative change (such as Schein, 2009; Bridges, 2009).

4. Approaches for supporting individuals throughout the change (including coaching and mentoring).

5. Leadership styles and typical barriers to leadership.

REFERENCES

Bridges, W., 2009. *Managing Transitions: making the most of change*. 3rd ed. London: Nicholas Brealey.

Cameron, E. and Green, M., 2012. *Making Sense of Change Management: a complete guide to the models, tools and techniques of organizational change*. 3rd ed. London: Kogan Page.

Chapman, J.A., 2002. A Framework For Transformational Change in Organizations. *Leadership & Organization Development Journal*, 23(1), pp.16–25 [online] Available at <http://www.emeraldinsight.com/0143-7739.htm> [Accessed 24 July 2013].

Roberto, M.A. and Levesque, L.C., 2005. The Art of Making Change Initiatives Stick. *MIT Sloan Management Review*, 46(4), SMR178, reprint no. 46410 [online] Available at: <http://www.sloanreview.mit.edu> [Accessed 26 July 2013].

Schein, E.H., 2009. *The Corporate Culture Survival Guide*. [ebook] San Francisco, CA: Jossey-Bass. Available at: Jossey Bass <http://www.josseybass.com> [Accessed 26 July 2013].

See also:

Knowledge Component 7.1: Building individual motivation to change

Knowledge Component 9.3: Behavioural change and coaching

Knowledge Component 12.1: Leadership principles

Knowledge Component 13.1: The Change Manager and Human Resources

Knowledge Component 11.3: Reinforcement systems

Changing behaviours to improve and sustain results

'One does not discover new lands without consenting to lose sight of the shore.'

Andre Gide.

DEFINITION

Reinforcement systems are a means for changing behaviour. Any change involves a departure from what is the norm. The purpose of reinforcement systems is to facilitate the transition, so new changes become an integral part of 'the way we do things around here'.

EXPLANATION

There are many ways to establish reinforcement systems. They range from:

- Putting rewards and incentives in place;

- Removing access to old ways of doing things to enforce compliance; to

- Providing direct feedback or additional support, such as mentoring or coaching.

The timing of behavioural reinforcement is a key consideration; the more immediate the feedback, the greater its impact.

Effective change managers help to clarify the desired new behaviours and link these directly to performance improvements and to the benefits expected from the change initiative. Positive reinforcement strategies motivate people more when they can see exactly how their changed behaviour leads to better results. Actively involving people in helping to embed change also increases motivation and helps to ensure change can be sustained.

Effective change managers focus on measuring and communicating these results at every available opportunity and highlight short-term successes as often as possible. This helps to instil confidence in the changes and shape people's attitudes and beliefs about them in a positive way.

Reinforcement systems are critical for embedding change. Effective change managers ensure appropriate reinforcement mechanisms are deployed on an on-going basis, and continuously monitor and evaluate them to ensure they remain effective.

KNOWLEDGE

The knowledge expected of an effective Change Manager is:

1. Types of reinforcement strategies (that means either financial or non-financial ones but also, for example, social ones) and the importance of the correct timing of these.

2. How to analyse behaviours to identify appropriate intervention strategies, and to evaluate outcomes of these strategies.

3. 'Systems thinking' to assess wider impact of intervention strategies, and how to use reinforcing loops.

4. Establishing feedback loops along with appropriate measures of performance.

5. The significance of the 'psychological contract'.

6. Continuous improvement concepts and models.

See also:

Knowledge Component 7.1: Building individual motivation to change

Knowledge Component 7.3: Planning for resistance

Knowledge Component 13.3: Process optimization in organizations

REFERENCES

Bridges, W., 2009. *Managing Transitions: making the most of change*. 3rd ed. London: Nicholas Brealey.

Cameron, E. and Green, M., 2012. *Making Sense of Change Management: a complete guide to the models, tools and techniques of organizational change*. 3rd ed. London: Kogan Page.

Cohen, D. S., 2008. *Make It Stick: Embedding Change in Organizational Culture*. In: *The Heart of Change Field Guide: Tools and Tactics for Leading Change in Your Organization*. Boston, MA: Harvard Business Press. Chapter 8.

Prosci, 2012. *Best Practices in Change Management*, Loveland, CO: Prosci. pp.98–100.

Roberto, M.A. and Levesque, L.C., 2005. The Art of Making Change Initiatives Stick. *MIT Sloan Management Review*, 46(4), SMR178, reprint no. 46410 [online] Available at: <http://www.sloanreview.mit.edu> [Accessed 26 July 2013].

Senge, P.M., 1993. *The Fifth Discipline: the art and practice of the learning organization*. London: Century.

Knowledge Component 11.4:
Achieving critical mass

Working towards a 'tipping point' for change

*'If you want to bring a fundamental change in people's belief and behavior...
you need to create a community around them, where those new beliefs can
be practiced and expressed and nurtured.'*

Malcolm Gladwell

DEFINITION

Within the context of organizational change initiatives, critical mass is
achieved when 'the people and systems operating in the new way achieve
unstoppable momentum' (Christopher Meyer, 2010). 'The tipping point is that
magic moment when an idea, trend, or social behaviour crosses a threshold,
tips, and spreads like wildfire' (Malcolm Gladwell, 2002).

EXPLANATION

Effective change managers recognize how achieving critical mass or a
'tipping point' helps drive change initiatives forward. It is not possible to
provide exact figures on what percentage of people in an organization would
constitute 'the minimum number required to sustain momentum' (critical
mass). It depends on the drivers for change, the nature of the change and the
environment within which change takes place.

At the outset of any change initiative there will be different levels of responses,
varying from enthusiastic support to strong resistance, and between these
sits indecisiveness. Typically, change initiatives begin with just a small
number of people who have that will and enthusiasm to drive the change
initiative forward ('innovators'). Once the messages around the change
initiative become clearer and there is some visible progress, others ('early
adopters') become willing to support and drive the change too. Effective
change managers focus on leveraging the interest of the early adopters to
influence 'the majority' across the organization.

They differentiate between the various interest groups and design effective
methods of communication and engagement to suit the different segments
of people. The extent to which this is done varies depending on the:

- Nature of change

- Timescales involved, and

- Different levels of compliance required.

Some change initiatives need full compliance and emotional buy-in for people to become 'true believers', while other types of change could potentially deliver organizational benefits with minimal levels of acceptance and compliance. Effective change managers focus their efforts on addressing and leveraging those key areas that will tip the balance towards achieving the greatest momentum for change.

KNOWLEDGE

The knowledge expected of an effective Change Manager is:

1. Concept of 'critical mass' and how to achieve it.

2. Signs of 'tipping points' and how to leverage them.

3. Behaviour patterns in adopting change (such as Everett Rogers' 'Diffusion of Innovation' theory).

REFERENCES

Gladwell, M., 2005. *The Tipping Point: how little things can make a big difference.* London: Abacus.

Meyer, C., 2010. *The Frontier of Change: Five Strategies to Accelerate Change to Critical Mass.* [pdf] Available at: <http://fastcycle.com/Articles/Five%20 Strategies%20to%20Accelerate%20Change.pdf> [Accessed 24 July 2013].

Nilakant, V. and Ramnarayan, S., 2006. *Change Management: altering mindsets in a global context.* New Delhi: Sage Publications.

Rogers, E.M., 2003. *Diffusion of Innovations.* 5th ed. New York, NY: Free Press.

Thaler, R.H. and Sunstein, C.R., 2008. *Nudge: improving decisions about health, wealth and happiness.* London: Yale University Press.

See also:

Knowledge Component 2.2: Drivers of change

Knowledge Component 5.2: Communicating change

Knowledge Component 7.1: Building individual motivation to change

Knowledge Component 12.6 Conflict management

Knowledge Component 11.5:
Embedding change

Empowering and motivating people to make change work

'Commitment means we haven't left ourselves an escape hatch.'

Charlotte Joko Beck

DEFINITION

Embedding change involves creating the conditions to enable people to take ownership of the changes while motivating and supporting them to adopt and integrate the required new ways of working.

EXPLANATION

Effective change managers monitor constantly to see how both the task and people aspects of embedding change are progressing. They introduce feedback loops so those responsible for ensuring change is adopted are aware of what is actually happening compared to what is expected.

If the expected outcomes from implementing changes are not achieved, the most likely cause is that people have not changed their behaviour. Monitoring this is key in tackling the problem. Although measurement alone will not produce the change in behaviours and attitudes required, measurement is critical in providing valuable feedback and pin-pointing the problem areas. Applying appropriate reinforcement systems to address and realign these problem areas ensures that change becomes institutionalized. Realignment involves activities such as redefining roles and changing the way people's performance is monitored and rewarded.

The measures identified will be specific to the change context and the desired changes. Change managers appreciate there are possible ripple effects and unintended consequences of measurement which also need to be considered.

Effective change managers help leaders and managers to create the conditions that empower and motivate people to take responsibility for embedding change. The factors contributing to change being embedded need to be considered and planned for at the outset of the change initiative.

KNOWLEDGE

The knowledge expected of an effective Change Manager is:

1. Models for institutionalizing change and realigning processes.

2. Approaches for identifying and monitoring key metrics on delivery of tasks and results obtained.

3. Designing measures for evaluating changes in behaviours and attitudes of people.

See also:

Knowledge Component 7.4: Measuring change effectiveness

Knowledge Component 9.3: Behavioural change and coaching

REFERENCES

Cabinet Office, 2011. *Managing Successful Programmes*. 4th ed. London: TSO.

Cameron, E. and Green, M., 2012. *Making Sense of Change Management: a complete guide to the models, tools and techniques of organizational change*. 3rd ed. London: Kogan Page.

Jenner, S., 2012. *Managing Benefits: optimizing the return from investments*. London: APMG-International, TSO.

Kotter, J.P., 1995. Leading Change: why transformation efforts fail. *Harvard Business Review*, May–June.

Roberto, M.A. and Levesque, L.C., 2005. The Art of Making Change Initiatives Stick. *MIT Sloan Management Review*, 46(4), SMR178, reprint no. 46410 [online] Available at: <http://www.sloanreview.mit.edu> [Accessed 26 July 2013].

Senge, P. et al., 1999. *The Dance Of Change: the challenge of sustaining momentum in learning organizations*. London: Nicholas Brealey.

12/

Knowledge Area 12: Personal and Professional Management

Developing personal effectiveness

BACKGROUND

A change management role can be extremely demanding. It requires high levels of personal commitment and resilience to remain motivated and perform well consistently throughout the change initiative. Having the skills to manage one's emotions and actions, while managing the emotional fallout and challenges of organizational change, requires deep inner resources and self-discipline. Developing skills in areas such as personal leadership and emotional intelligence equips change managers with the resources required – not only to develop resilience but also to manage themselves more effectively and to lead others by example.

Change managers are instrumental in leading the way and developing high-performing change teams, who have the shared sense of purpose and motivation needed to deliver successful change. The development of strong interpersonal communication, effective influencing, negotiation and conflict management skills means they have a wide array of personal approaches and strategies available for dealing with diverse groups of people at all levels of the organization. These skills give them the flexibility and confidence to deal with the tough challenges that arise during any change initiative.

By focusing on both the personal and professional management aspects of their development, effective change managers create the optimum conditions for success for themselves and for the organization.

KNOWLEDGE COMPONENTS

These Knowledge Components are essential for developing personal and professional management skills:

1. Leadership principles

2. Building team effectiveness

3. Emotional intelligence

4. Effective influence

5. Negotiation

6. Conflict management

PERSONAL AND PROFESSIONAL MANAGEMENT IN PRACTICE

A critical aspect of a change manager's role is engaging with people to exchange information, gain their support, facilitate collaboration, help resolve issues over conflicting interests and negotiate agreements. This must all be accomplished while navigating their way through the challenges of working in complex environments, to deliver change and meet organizational objectives. Effective change managers are resilient and highly effective at managing themselves, in order to be able to lead and influence others effectively throughout the change initiative. They are self-aware and recognize the importance of investing time in their own development. Change managers also focus their efforts on building highly effective teams and creating the right environment for them to ensure the best chances of success.

HOW THIS KNOWLEDGE AREA SUPPORTS
THE CMI CHANGE MANAGEMENT PRACTITIONER COMPETENCIES

Related Change Manager Practitioner Competencies	12.1 Leadership principles	12.2 Building team effectiveness	12.3 Emotional intelligence	12.4 Effective influence	12.5 Negotiation	12.6 Conflict management
Facilitating Change	O		O	O		O
Strategic Thinking				O	O	O
Thinking & Judgement	O				O	O
Influencing Others	O	O	O	O	O	O
Coaching for Change	O	O	O	O		
Project Management	O	O		O	O	O
Communication Skills	O	O	O	O	O	O
Self Management			O			
Facilitation			O	O		O
Specialist Expertise – Learning & Development	O	O	O	O		O
Specialist Expertise – Communication	O		O	O		O

KEY REFERENCES FOR THIS KNOWLEDGE AREA

Cameron, E. and Green, M., 2012. *Making Sense of Change Management: a complete guide to the models, tools and techniques of organizational change.* 3rd ed. London: Kogan Page. Chapter 5 and pp.166–174.

Covey, S.R., 2011. *The 7 Habits of Highly Effective People.* Export ed. NY: Simon & Schuster.

Goleman, D., 2000. Leadership that Gets Results. *Harvard Business Review,* March–April, 78(2), pp.78–90.

Knowledge Component 12.1:
Leadership principles

Effective leadership styles and approaches

'Leadership requires as much courage as it does insight.'

Lencioni

DEFINITION

Leadership is defined as 'a process of social influence in which one person is able to enlist the aid and support of others in the accomplishment of a common task' (Chemers, 2000).

EXPLANATION

Effective change managers provide leadership throughout the change initiative, both for those over whom they may have line authority, and for those over whom they have no such authority. Their ability to build relationships, to engage with people and to influence them in order to gain their support for a shared purpose is what helps to drive change initiatives forward.

Any change initiative is challenging and unlikely to go smoothly, so change managers need to be resilient and remain calm under pressure. They are self-aware, recognize their strengths and weaknesses, and continue to learn and enhance their skills.

Increasingly, organizations are facing change with greater levels of uncertainty and complexity. This needs people to work in a more collaborative and open environment, to be able to share and learn from each other as solutions emerge. Effective change managers are comfortable dealing with ambiguity and skilled in facilitating people through this. The approach and style of leadership they adopt will vary depending on the situation and their level of power and influence within the organization.

Change managers also focus on supporting other leaders involved in the change initiative. As such, they recognize where ineffective leadership behaviours of others may inhibit progress, and support those leaders in developing their change leadership effectiveness.

The Change Management Institute

KNOWLEDGE

The knowledge expected of an effective Change Manager is:

1. Perspectives on different approaches to:

   - Leadership (for example visionary, transformational, adaptive and connective); and
   - Managing organizational change (such as programmatic approaches and participative processes (see Beer and Nohria, 2000).

2. Different leadership styles and how to adapt leadership styles appropriately to the situation, the nature of the change involved and the culture of the organization.

3. Principles of inner and outer leadership and how to develop these skills.

4. Problem-solving and creative thinking.

5. Strategies for developing personal effectiveness and resilience.

See also:

Knowledge Component 1.4: Key roles in organizational change

Knowledge Component 7.1: Building individual motivation to change

REFERENCES

Beer, M. and Nohria, N., 2000. Cracking the Code of Change. *Harvard Business Review,* May-June.

Cameron, E. and Green, M., 2008. *Making Sense of Leadership: exploring the five key roles used by effective leaders.* London: Kogan Page.

Cameron, E. and Green, M., 2012. *Making Sense of Change Management: a complete guide to the models, tools and techniques of organizational change.* 3rd ed. London: Kogan Page. pp.82–85.

Chemers, M.M., 2000. Leadership Research and Theory: a functional integration. *Group Dynamics: Theory, Research and Practice,* 4(1), pp.27–43.

Covey, S.R., 2011. *The 7 Habits of Highly Effective People.* Export ed. NY: Simon & Schuster.

George, W., Sims, P., McLean, A.N. and Mayer, D., 2007. Discovering Your Authentic Leadership. *Harvard Business Review,* February, 85(2), pp.129–138.

Goleman, D., 2000. Leadership that Gets Results. *Harvard Business Review,* March–April, 78(2), pp.78–90.

Heifetz, A. and Laurie, L.L., 2001. The Work of Leadership. *Harvard Business Review,* December, 79(11), pp.131–140.

Kanter, R.M., 2003. *Leadership for Change: Enduring Skills for Change Masters* (Harvard Business Review Case Study, 9-304-062). [pdf] Available at: <http://hbr.org/product/leadership-for-change-enduring-skills-for-change-m/an/304062-PDF-ENG> [Accessed 20 July 2013]

Rock, D., 2009. *Your Brain at Work: strategies for overcoming distraction, regaining focus, and working smarter all day long.* New York, NY: HarperCollins Publishers.

Senge, P.M., 1993. *The Fifth Discipline: the art and practice of the learning organization.* London: Century.

Knowledge Component 12.2:
Building team effectiveness

The need for a range of teams during change

'The greater the loyalty of a group toward the group, the greater is the motivation among the members to achieve the goals of the group, and the greater the probability that the group will achieve its goals.'

Rensis Likert

DEFINITION

Building team effectiveness means developing teams that have a strong and shared sense of purpose, who plan and organize their work around that purpose and foster an atmosphere of openness and trust, so they can perform at an optimum level.

EXPLANATION

Effective change managers consider how to set up the most appropriate types and combinations of teams during a change initiative, those that will ensure the best chances of success. Many different types of teams can be established during the course of a change initiative, including project teams, network teams, focus groups and task forces.

During the early days of a change initiative, there may be a single change team. As change progresses, however, the number of different teams involved is likely to increase quite rapidly. As people in the organization see the teams delivering tangible results, their level of confidence in the teams will increase, which helps to build greater commitment to the change initiative across the organization.

Change managers support and guide teams throughout the change initiative, helping them to mature from 'just formed' to 'highly performing', so that they can:

- Develop a strong and shared sense of purpose;

- Engage with their stakeholders and other teams within the change initiative;

- Stay on track with their approach and direction;

- Develop a climate of trust and commitment within the teams;

- Put clear processes in place for dealing with issues and making decisions;

- Encourage collaborative working with full participation; and

- Create open flows of communication among and between teams.

It is rare for all teams within a change initiative to be located in one place. They are more likely to be distributed across different locations. Frequently the members of any one team are also drawn from different geographical locations. Focusing on developing team effectiveness and skills becomes increasingly important in this virtual team environment.

KNOWLEDGE

The knowledge expected of an effective Change Manager is:

See also:

Knowledge Component 1.3: Change and the organization

1. Key factors that contribute to a team's effectiveness and that help to diagnose problems in dysfunctional teams.

2. Different types of organizational teams, their advantages and disadvantages in supporting organizational change.

3. Changing dynamics of teams (see Tuckman and Jensen, 1977), and the different leadership characteristics required through the phases of team maturity.

4. Approaches for managing virtual teams.

REFERENCES

Adair, J., 2009. *Effective Team Building: how to make a winning team*. Revised ed. London: Pan Books.

Cameron, E. and Green, M., 2012. *Making Sense of Change Management: a complete guide to the models, tools and techniques of organizational change*. 3rd ed. London: Kogan Page.

Cohen, D. S., 2005. Build Guiding Teams: Creating a Climate for Change. In: *The Heart of Change Field Guide: Tools and Tactics for Leading Change in Your Organization*. Boston, Massachusetts: Harvard Business Press.

Katzenbach, J.R. and Smith, D.K., 2005. *The Wisdom of Teams: creating the high-performance organization*. Berkshire: McGraw-Hill.

Lencioni, P., 2002. *The Five Dysfunctions of a Team: a leadership fable*. San Francisco, CA: Jossey-Bass.

Prosci, 2012. *Best Practices in Change Management*, Loveland, CO: Prosci. pp.33–40.

Tuckman, B.W. and Jensen, M.A., 1977. Stages of Small-Group Development Revisited. *Group and Organization Studies,* 2(4), pp.419–427.

Knowledge Component 12.3: Emotional intelligence

The importance of strong emotional competencies in dealing with change

'The emotional brain responds to an event more quickly than the thinking brain.'

Daniel Goleman

DEFINITION

'Emotional intelligence is a type of social intelligence that involves the ability to monitor one's own and others' emotions, to discriminate among them and to use the information to guide one's thinking and actions' (Salovey and Mayer, 1990).

EXPLANATION

Change managers who demonstrate strong emotional competencies are more effective in dealing with the challenges that are inevitable during any change – particularly the people and emotional aspects of change.

Effective change managers are self-aware, can manage their own emotions and deal with the emotions of others as well. Being able to use appropriate interpersonal skills allows change managers to influence others more. This results in lower levels of anxiety or stress during change, both for themselves and for others around them.

They recognize early warning signals of unhelpful emotions and step in to deal with these effectively before issues escalate to a point where progress of the change initiative is hindered. Developing emotional intelligence also helps to build personal resilience, which is essential for coping with the challenges of bringing about successful change.

An essential aspect of the change manager's role is to build relationships and form coalitions of support for the change initiative, across diverse stakeholder groups with potentially conflicting views. This requires effective social skill, defined as 'the ability to move people in the direction required' (Goleman, 1997). This is one of the core emotional competencies, along with self-awareness, self-management and social awareness.

Effective change managers can support teams in developing their emotional intelligence through coaching. This helps to improve team effectiveness and reduce potential for conflict.

KNOWLEDGE

The knowledge expected of an effective Change Manager is:

1. Principles of emotional and social intelligence.

2. Characteristics of emotional competency areas, including self-awareness, self-management, social awareness and social skills (see Goleman, 1997).

3. Recognizing strengths and weaknesses in self and others and developing resilience.

4. Approaches for developing emotional competencies in self and in others.

REFERENCES

Balogun, J. and Hailey, V.H., 2008. *Exploring Strategic Change.* 3rd ed. Harlow, Essex: Pearson Education.

Cameron, E. and Green, M., 2012. *Making Sense of Change Management: a complete guide to the models, tools and techniques of organizational change.* 3rd ed. London: Kogan Page. pp.174–186.

Goleman, D., 1997. What Makes a Leader? *Harvard Business Review*, January, 85(2), pp.1–21.

Goleman, D., 1998. *Working with Emotional Intelligence.* New York: Bantam Books.

Jordan, P.J., 2009. Dealing With Organizational Change: can emotional intelligence enhance organizational learning? *International Journal of Organizational Behaviour*, 8(1), pp.456–471.

Mersino, A.C., 2007. *Emotional Intelligence for Project Managers: the people skills you need to achieve outstanding results*, New York, NY: AMACOM/American Management Association.

Salovey, P. and Mayer, J.D., 1990. *Emotional Intelligence.* University of New Hampshire. [pdf] Available at: <http://www.unh.edu/emotional_intelligence/EIAssets/EmotionalIntelligenceProper/EI1990%20Emotional%20Intelligence.pdf> [Accessed 27 July 2013].

For those who find the Myers-Briggs Type Indicator® (MBTI®) helpful, there is an associated brief online resource about resilience. It contains helpful information which goes beyond the specific links with MBTI®:

Hackston, J. and Moyle, P., 2013. *Stressed Out?! Our quick guide to building resilience.* [online] Available at: <http://www.opp.com/en/solutions/stress-management/quickguidetoresilience?utm_medium=email&utm_source=OPP+Ltd&utm_campaign=3128464_Version_2_OPPinions&dm_t=0,0,0,0,0#.UkVqbrlwbGg> [Accessed 27 September 2013].

See also:

Knowledge Component 4.3: Managing relationships and mobilizing stakeholders

Knowledge Component 5.1: Theory of effective communicating

Knowledge Component 9.3: Behavioural change and coaching

Knowledge Component 12.4:
Effective Influence

Using influencing skills through effective collaboration

'If you want to build a ship, don't drum up the men to gather wood, divide the work and give orders. Instead, teach them to yearn for the vast and endless sea.'

Antoine de Saint-Exupery

DEFINITION

Influence is defined as 'a force one person (the agent) exerts on someone else (the target) to induce a change in the target, including changes in behaviours, opinions, attitudes, goals, needs and values' and 'the ability to affect the behaviour of others in a particular direction' (French and Raven, 1959).

EXPLANATION

The ability to influence people in order to facilitate change is a critical skill for change managers. It is possible to influence through power and direct authority but most of the people with whom change managers interact to gain support or to progress change in some way are people over whom they have no direct authority. As a result, influencing through more collaborative means is likely to be more effective. Change managers need to establish their credibility to improve their effectiveness in exerting influence.

Developing rapport and adapting behaviours to match others, are important steps towards influencing. Understanding what motivates people, seeing their perspective, listening attentively and using language that matches their frames of reference are also important contributors to effective influencing.

Effective change managers recognize the need to adopt different strategies and tactics, depending on the people involved and on the situation. For example, some people need reasoned logic and facts, while others respond better to an approach that is appealing to their values or emotions. It could be a simple transactional exchange of favours, which is mutually beneficial to either side, or a more coercive approach, demanding full compliance.

KNOWLEDGE

The knowledge expected of an effective Change Manager is:

1. Concepts of the psychology of compliance and influence (for example Robert Cialdini's 'six principles of influence').

2. A range of approaches and models for influencing.

3. Common 'push and pull' tactics for influencing – their advantages and disadvantages.

4. Recognizing outcomes from influencing behaviours (such as resistance, compliance or commitment) and knowing how to respond to these.

5. Approaches for developing rapport and effective communication skills.

6. Differences between *power* and *influence*.

7. Sources of power.

See also:

Knowledge Component 5.1: Theory of effective communicating

Knowledge Component 7.1: Building individual motivation to change

Knowledge Component 9.3: Behavioural change and coaching

REFERENCES

Cialdini, R.B., 2006. *Influence: the psychology of persuasion*. New York, NY: Harper Business.

Borg, J., 2007. *Persuasion: the art of influencing people*. 2nd ed. Harlow, Essex: Pearson Education.

French, J.P.R. and Raven, B., 1959. The bases of social power. In: D. Cartwright, ed., *Studies in social power*. 7th ed. Ann Arbor: University of Michigan, Institute for Social Research.

Fritz, S., Brown, W., Lunde, J. and Banset, E., 1999. *Interpersonal Skills for Leadership*. 2nd ed. Upper Saddle River, NJ: Prentice Hall.

Hughes, R., Ginnett, R. and Curphy, G., 1995. Power, influence and influence tactics. In: J. Thomas Wren, ed., 1995. *The Leader's Companion*. New York, NY: The Free Press.

Yukl, G. and Falbe, C., 1990. Influence Tactics and Objectives in Upward, Downward and Lateral Influence Attempts. *Journal of Applied Psychology*, 75(2), pp.132–140.

Knowledge Component 12.5:
Negotiation

Facilitating agreement among others

'Let us never negotiate out of fear. But let us never fear to negotiate.'

John F. Kennedy

DEFINITION

Negotiation 'is a two-way communication to reach an agreement when both parties have a combination of shared and opposed interest' (Fisher and Ury, 1991). Negotiations are a 'vehicle of communication and stakeholder management. As such, they play a vital role in assisting to obtain a better grasp of the complex issues, factors and human dynamics behind important issues' (Alfredson and Cungu, 2008).

EXPLANATION

During any change initiative, problems arise due to people having differing interests and conflicting needs. Effective change managers adopt suitable approaches to negotiation, depending on the type of situation they are dealing with, to overcome conflict and facilitate agreement among others.

For successful negotiation, a precondition is that the parties involved are committed to reaching agreement, in a way that benefits all concerned. This enables the relationship between the parties to continue in a productive way.

Change managers ensure:

- The focus is on the problem and not on the people or personalities involved;

- All parties acknowledge and understand there is common interest among them;

- Each party sees the problem from the other's perspective as well as clarifying their own position to clearly understand the key issues and the criteria to be met;

- All parties generate possible solutions together to achieve the desired results;

- All parties agree on a solution that meets the criteria of all parties; and

- Appropriate authority or delegated powers – such as senior management or other sources – back up the decisions agreed on.

Cultural considerations must also be taken into account when negotiating. There can be differences in terminology used, also in beliefs and attitudes, and perhaps even in social etiquette. These could become barriers to successful negotiation if they are not recognized and addressed on time. Applying the factors above helps to maintain transparency and clarity of the objective.

If cultural differences or very diverse groups are involved, then frequently checking that there is shared understanding is even more important.

KNOWLEDGE

The knowledge expected of an effective Change Manager is:

1. Approaches for negotiating (such as soft, hard and principled) and the basic concepts of each approach.

2. The stages involved in negotiation (pre-negotiation, actual negotiations and post-negotiation).

3. Awareness of different negotiation strategies and when it is appropriate to use them.

4. Cultural impacts on negotiation strategies.

5. Potential barriers to successful negotiation.

See also:

Knowledge Component 5.1: Theory of effective communicating

REFERENCES

Alfredson, T. and Cungu, A., 2008. *Negotiation Theory and Practice: a review of the literature.* [pdf] Available at: <http://www.fao.org/docs/up/easypol/550/4-5_negotiation_background_paper_179en.pdf> [Accessed 31 July 2013].

Fisher, R. and Ury, W., 1999. *Getting to Yes: negotiating an agreement without giving in.* 2nd ed. London: Random House.

Verma, V.K.,1996. *Human Resource Skills for the Project Manager: the human aspects of project management.* Volume 2. Sylva, NC: Project Management Institute. p.172.

Knowledge Component 12.6: Conflict Management

Overcome conflict to secure mutually beneficial agreements

'It is possible to conceive conflict as not necessarily a wasteful outbreak of incompatibilities, but a normal process by which socially valuable differences register themselves for the enrichment of all concerned.'

Mary Parker Follett

DEFINITION

Managing conflict involves 'designing effective strategies to minimize the dysfunctions of conflict and enhance the constructive functions of conflict in order to enhance learning and effectiveness in an organization' (Rahim, 2002).

EXPLANATION

Change managers are frequently faced with conflict situations that need resolving to avoid unnecessary delays to the change initiative. There will be more conflict in environments with higher levels of uncertainty and ambiguity, more diverse groups of stakeholders, unclear priorities and tight resource constraints.

Effective change managers can anticipate disruptive conflict, and find timely resolutions against it. However, conflict is not always negative – it can be used for generating more creativity and improving the quality of decisions. So, if the conflict brings a positive influence, effective change managers find ways to maximize the opportunities it presents.

Effective change managers focus on finding the causes of the conflict – not only the symptoms – and consider the following factors for choosing appropriate responses to address them:

- Intensity of the conflict and its impact on the people involved; and

- Criticality in terms of time available and the impact on progress of the change initiative.

Change managers play an important role in fostering an environment where people are comfortable to highlight potential conflict situations and are proactive in dealing with conflict. To do this effectively, change managers must themselves be comfortable with conflict and develop appropriate personal strategies for dealing with it. They must also appreciate the limits of their influence and know when to seek guidance or involvement of those with the appropriate authority – depending on the situation this may include senior management or human resources.

KNOWLEDGE

The knowledge expected of an effective Change Manager is:

1. Recognizing different types of conflict (such as 'functional conflict' and 'relational conflict').

2. Understanding potential sources of conflict (such as individual and organizational), and how to address the underlying causes.

3. Understanding the difference between 'conflict resolution' and 'conflict management'.

4. Maximizing the positive aspects of conflict;

5. Using different styles for conflict resolution (such as 'smoothing', 'forcing', 'withdrawal', 'compromising' and 'collaborating').

6. Applying approaches and models for dealing with different types of conflict (see Kilmann, 2011).

See also:

Knowledge Component 4.3: Managing relationships and mobilizing stakeholders

Knowledge Component 5.1: Theory of effective communicating

Knowledge Component 7.3: Planning for resistance

REFERENCES

Kilmann, R.H., 2011. *Celebrating 40 Years with the TKI Assessment: a summary of my favourite insights.* [pdf] Available at: https://www.cpp.com/PDFs/Author_Insights_April_2011.pdf> [Accessed 20 August 2013].

MindTools.com. *Conflict Resolution: resolving conflict rationally and effectively.* [online] Available at: <http://www.mindtools.com/pages/article/newLDR_81.htm> [Accessed 28 July 2013].

Rahim, M.A., 2002. Toward a Theory of Managing Organizational Conflict. *International Journal of Conflict Management,* [e-journal] 13(3). [online] <http://papers.ssrn.com/sol3/papers.cfm?abstract_id=437684> [Accessed 31 July 2013].

Verma, V.K., 1996. *Human Resource Skills for the Project Manager: the human aspects of project management.* Volume 2. Sylva, NC: Project Management Institute.

13/

Knowledge Area 13: Organizational Considerations

Critical elements of awareness for professional Change Managers

BACKGROUND

This Knowledge Area brings together a range of matters outside the discipline of change management of which effective change managers should have awareness. These matters are clearly the responsibility of the organization, and change managers are not required to have specialist expertise in them. However, complete lack of awareness on the part of the change manager may endanger change initiatives if, as a result of a 'blind spot', specialist support is not alerted or sought.

UK research by the Chartered Institute for Personnel and Development (CIPD) indicates that the failure rate in change initiatives is as high as 60% where reorganization is involved. The effective change manager knows that awareness of Human Resources (HR) issues, as well as early and continuous involvement of HR professionals can contribute to a successful change initiative and avoid potential legal pitfalls.

Related environmental protection, occupational health and safety at work (referred to in this document as 'SHE' – Safety, Health and Environment, but commonly also referred to as HSE, EHS or OH&S) are also key considerations. Effective change managers can see the SHE implications of change initiatives and ensure that these are properly evaluated by those with appropriate training.

Many organizations have a focus on continuous improvement, 'Lean' or 'Six Sigma' approaches to optimizing processes. Effective change managers are familiar with the major approaches used.

The financial viability of a change initiative is a critical indicator of the likelihood of a successful outcome. Effective change managers understand the principles of sound financial management. They are particularly aware of the importance of testing the viability and achievability of the investment case for change, and have an adequate working understanding of other basic financial concepts used in organizations.

KNOWLEDGE COMPONENTS

These Knowledge Components represent some important organizational considerations for change managers to be aware of:

1. The Change Manager and Human Resources

2. Safety, health and environment issues in change

3. Process optimization in organizations

4. Financial management for change managers

ORGANIZATIONAL CONSIDERATIONS IN PRACTICE

Effective change managers are not experts in all management disciplines but will have an awareness of several key non-change management aspects of organizational functions which may have an impact on a change initiative. This includes securing the early and continuous involvement of Human Resources (HR) professionals to ensure employee engagement (intellectual, affective and social) is achieved and the impact of change on them has a 'voice'.

Change managers also know that change can create 'abnormal operating conditions' for a time. They work with the appropriate disciplines to ensure that local policies and procedures for Safety, Health and Environment issues (SHE) are taken into account and applied when planning and implementing change.

A frequent requirement in a change initiative is the mapping of organizational business and process flows and interactions. Effective change managers are familiar with different mapping methods and techniques and attend workshops with business and process analysts and key business area experts to contribute to their creation and use, for example in conducting impact assessments or identification of process change that will result in benefits.

Effective change managers understand the principles and practices of sound cost and financial management to determine the viability of a change initiative. They work with business and finance specialists to build a convincing business case for change and with programme and project managers to maintain a continuous focus on cost-effectiveness and the achievement of financial goals.

HOW THIS KNOWLEDGE AREA SUPPORTS
THE CMI CHANGE MANAGEMENT PRACTITIONER COMPETENCIES

Related Change Manager Practitioner Competencies	13.1 The Change Manager and HR	13.2 Safety health and environment issues in change	13.3 Process optimization in organizations	13.4 Financial Management for change managers
Facilitating Change				O
Strategic Thinking			O	
Thinking & Judgement			O	O
Coaching for Change	O		O	
Project Management			O	O

KEY REFERENCES FOR THIS KNOWLEDGE AREA

Cabinet Office, 2010. *Management of Value*. London: TSO.

Cabinet Office, 2011. *Managing Successful Programmes*. 4th ed. London: TSO.

Cummings, T.G. and Worley, C.G., 2009. *Organization Development and Change*. 9th ed. Mason, OH: South-Western Publishing.

George, M.L., Rowlands, D., Price, M. and Maxey, J., 2005. *The Lean Six Sigma Pocket Tool Book*. New York: McGraw Hill. Chapter 3.

Jenner, S., 2012. *Managing Benefits: optimizing the return from investments*. London: APMG-International, TSO.

Stanford, N., 2007. *Guide to Organisation Design: creating high performing and adaptable enterprises*. London: Economist Books.

Knowledge Component 13.1: The Change Manager and Human Resources

Working with HR professionals beyond traditional organizational models

'Organization doesn't really accomplish anything. Plans don't accomplish anything, either. Theories of management don't much matter. Endeavours succeed or fail because of the people involved. Only by attracting the best people will you accomplish great deeds.'

Colin Powell

DEFINITION

Human Resources (HR) functions exist to support the line management of the organization in making the most effective use of the people who work for it, and doing so in an appropriate and professional manner which recognizes the needs of those people as well. HR is frequently charged with recruitment, selection, learning and development (HRD), talent management, organization design, employee engagement, termination of employment, compliance with employee legislation and employee relations (sometimes called Industrial Relations or 'IR'). Change initiatives frequently interface with a number of these issues.

EXPLANATION

Effective change managers know that an awareness of HR issues – and the early and continuous involvement of HR professionals – is often a critical success factor for a change initiative. This is especially relevant when the initiative includes an element of reorganization. Such reorganizations frequently move away from traditional forms of organization to emerging models where, for example, 'project working' and virtual structures are becoming common. These present the change manager with particular challenges, such as information sharing and communications.

Effective employee engagement is a major contributor to organizational 'health' and to individual job satisfaction and performance. Employee engagement (intellectual, affective and social) is essential to a successful change initiative. In all these areas the contribution of the organization's HR function is likely to be essential.

Effective change managers know how an effective relationship with the HR function can improve the likelihood of a successful change initiative:

- Securing early involvement of HR professionals in the project team to address people issues and skills and competency needs, as well as the wider, organizational structure;

- Using the specialist skills and knowledge of HR professionals when assessing the impact of change on people, communicating (giving people a 'voice') and addressing specific concerns and resistance to change; and

- Ensuring that specific organization development goals are aligned with broader strategic goals, including workforce planning.

KNOWLEDGE

The knowledge expected of an effective Change Manager is:

1. Awareness of local legislative frameworks, statutes, regulations and policies which govern employment, equality and diversity.

2. Awareness of the organization's HR policies and procedures, including people development, engagement, performance management and employee relations (sometimes called 'industrial relations' or 'IR').

3. Awareness of the organization's employee relations policies and agreements (including guidelines for managing conflict).

4. Principles of organization design (including different organizational forms, models and structures).

See also:

Knowledge Area 4: Stakeholder Strategy

Knowledge Area 5: Communication and Engagement

Knowledge Area 7: Change Readiness, Planning and Measurement

Knowledge Component 12.6: Conflict management

REFERENCES

Cannon, J.A. and McGee, R., 2008. *Organisational Development and Change: CIPD toolkit.* London: CIPD.

Cummings, T.G. and Worley, C.G., 2009. *Organization Development and Change.* 9th ed. Mason, OH: South-Western Publishing.

Department for Business Innovation & Skills, 2013. *The 2011 Workplace Employment Relations Study (WERS).*

Nadler, D.A., Gerstein, M.C. and Shaw, R.B., 1992. *Organizational Architecture: designs for changing organizations.* San Francisco, CA: Jossey Bass.

Knowledge Component 13.2:
Safety, health and environment issues in change

Recognizing the implications for safety, health and the environment of 'abnormal operating conditions' arising from change

'Concern for man himself and his safety must always form the chief interest of all technical endeavours.'

Albert Einstein

DEFINITION

Safety, Health and Environment issues (SHE – also known as EHS, Health and Safety, Occupational Health & Safety (OH&S) and other acronyms) are a critical aspect of the legal and regulatory framework within which organizations operate.

EXPLANATION

Effective change managers know that local policies and procedures for SHE must be taken into account when planning and implementing change. The greatest risks to SHE typically result from 'abnormal operating conditions' such as those often experienced when an organization is undergoing change. However, consideration must also be given to the likely consequences to the SHE issues which will result from the successful implementation of a change initiative. Effective change managers seek appropriate professional advice throughout the process of specifying, initiating, implementing and embedding the change, to ensure that good practice is followed at every stage.

See also:

Knowledge Component 2.3: Change Definition

Knowledge Area 6: Change impact

Knowledge Area 8: Project Management

Knowledge Component 11.5: Embedding change

KNOWLEDGE

The knowledge expected of an effective Change Manager is:

1. An awareness of local SHE legal requirements, and the organization's related policies and management systems.

2. The scope and purpose of SHE and how these impact on organizational change.

3. An awareness of common SHE assessment methods, such as 'plan–do–check–act' or 'plan–do–check–adjust' (PDCA) or 'observe–plan–do–check–act' (OPDCA).
   (These methods are also known as the 'plan–do–study–act' (PDSA) method, 'Deming circle', 'Deming cycle', 'Deming wheel', 'Shewhart cycle', and 'control circle' or 'control cycle'.)

REFERENCES

Clutterbuck, D., 2003. *Managing Work–Life Balance: a guide for HR in achieving organisational and individual change.* London: CIPD.

Deming, E.W., 1986. *Out of the Crisis.* MIT Center for Advanced Engineering Study.

Stranks, J., 2008. *Health And Safety At Work: an essential guide for managers.* 8th ed. London: Kogan Page.

Further information about these issues is also to be found on the website of the Premier Association for EHS Management (NAEM) at <www.naem.org>.

Knowledge Component 13.3:
Process optimization in organizations

Using process mapping to inform change strategy, approach, benefits and risks

'The system is that there is no system. That doesn't mean we don't have process. Apple is a very disciplined company, and we have great processes. But that's not what it's about. Process makes you more efficient.'

Steve Jobs

DEFINITION

The term 'process optimization' covers the range of approaches used by organizations to analyse and improve their business processes. These include Total Quality Management (TQM), Continuous Improvement (CI), Lean and Six Sigma. The focus of process optimization is to improve control of the organization's processes across departmental structures, and to identify and remove wasteful elements.

EXPLANATION

An important aspect of a change initiative is often the mapping of organizational business and process flows and interactions. These maps form a critical input for the change manager's impact assessments and inform change strategy and approach. Effective change managers are familiar with some commonly used ways of mapping and analysing business processes. Process mapping helps to identify sequence and stages of process activities and tasks and is used extensively in 'lean' thinking, particularly in manufacturing and service operations. It is used to identify potential improvements (benefits) in delivering value to its customers. This is also referred to as the 'value proposition'.

Effective change managers do not have to be expert practitioners in process mapping but know how to apply the specialist skills of those trained in these disciplines.

KNOWLEDGE

The knowledge expected of an effective Change Manager is:

1. The relevance and value of mapping current ('as is') and future state ('to be') processes, including both

   - the value of the maps themselves, and
   - the value of engaging stakeholders in the mapping process.

2. The technique for creating some of the simpler process maps to be used with stakeholder groups.

3. Interpretation of common process maps:

   - To identify risks and opportunities for improvements, and
   - As a source of information for impact assessments.

4. The value that specialists trained in Lean, Six Sigma or other disciplines can bring to process mapping and optimization.

See also:

Knowledge Component 2.3: Change definition

Knowledge Area 3: Managing Benefits

Knowledge Area 4: Stakeholder Strategy

Knowledge Component 6.1: Assessing the impact of change

Knowledge Component 6.2: Assessing and managing the risks of change

REFERENCES

Businessballs.com. *Business Process Modelling – business process modelling explanation – diagrams, definitions, examples:* www.businessballs.com/business-process-modelling.htm

Cabinet Office, 2010. *Management of Value*. London: TSO.

Deming, E.W., 1986. *Out of the Crisis*. MIT Center for Advanced Engineering Study.

Hammer, M., 1997. *Beyond Re-engineering: how the process-centered organisation is changing our work and our lives*. New York: HarperCollins.

Hild, C., Sanders, D. and Ross B., 1999. The Thought Map. *Quality Engineering,* 12(1), pp.21–27.

Sanders, D., Ross, W. and Coleman, J., 1999. The Process Map. *Quality Engineering,* 11(4), pp.555–561.

Knowledge component 13.4:
Financial management for
change managers

Understanding the principles of cost management and investment in change

'Being good in business is the most fascinating kind of art. Making money is art and working is art and good business is the best art.'

Andy Warhol

DEFINITION

Financial management includes the systems for recording, reporting, planning and controlling an organization's financial resources. It includes methods to evaluate change initiatives and projects, and to monitor and assess their value.

EXPLANATION

The financial viability of a change initiative is a critical indicator of the likelihood of a successful outcome. Effective change managers understand the principles and practices of sound cost and financial management in a change initiative. This focuses particularly on establishing (and regularly reviewing) the viability and achievability of the investment case for change. At project level the task of cost and financial management belongs to the portfolio, programme or project manager. It is common for a large or complex change initiative to appoint an accountant to manage the financial aspects of the change. However, effective change managers are familiar with estimating and investment appraisal methods and techniques. A particular focus for the change manager will be the identification and quantification (and, later, monitoring, measuring and tracking) of benefits and dis-benefits for a change initiative. This also includes ensuring that the business case for a change initiative reflects the full cost of change.

Effective change managers can evaluate a change initiative through:

- Understanding the relevance and importance of evaluating the financial viability and achievability of a change initiative;

- Being aware how to make best use of suitably qualified financial management practitioners (such as accountants);

- Understanding how to select appropriate financial and cost-benefit criteria; and

- Being aware of common methods and techniques for cost estimating and investment appraisal, and for quantifying benefits and their negative effects.

KNOWLEDGE

The knowledge expected of an effective Change Manager is:

1. The difference between 'revenue' and 'capital expenditure'.

2. How an organization uses budgets to manage its costs (including methods of forecasting and of budget variance analysis).

3. The reasons for, and appropriate uses of, a financial appraisal of a proposed change initiative.

4. An awareness of the time value of money, including the principles behind commonly-used methods of investment appraisal.

5. Appropriate financial and cost-benefit criteria, including the principles behind common ways of valuing benefits and negative effects.

6. The concept of 'leading and lagging indicators', and its significance.

REFERENCES

Cabinet Office, 2010. *Management of Value*. London: TSO.

Cabinet Office, 2011. *Management of Portfolios*. London: TSO.

Cabinet Office, 2011. *Managing Successful Programmes*. 4th ed. London: TSO.

Jenner, S., 2012. *Managing Benefits: optimizing the return from investments*. London: APMG-International, TSO.

Project Management Institute, 2013. *A Guide to the Project Management Body of Knowledge (PMBOK® Guide)*. 5th ed. Newtown Square, PA: The Project Management Institute.

See also:

Knowledge Component 2.3: Change definition

Knowledge Area 3: Managing Benefits

Knowledge Component 6.1: Assessing the impact of change

Knowledge Area 8: Project Management

Appendix A
The CMI Organizational Change Management Maturity Model and the CMBoK

This initial release of the CMI CMBoK focuses primarily on the 'project' level of change management capability within the CMI Organizational Change Management Maturity Model although many of the concepts are relevant to all levels. Over time we expect to incorporate the feedback we receive to expand on the specific knowledge underpinning change management practice in the 'business' and 'organizational' levels of capability. The table below summarises how the CMBoK relates to all three maturity levels:

CMBoK Knowledge Area	Project	Business	Organization
1/ **A Change Management Perspective**	Concepts that are influential in introducing a change	Concepts that are relevant to a business undergoing frequent change	Concepts that relate to a complex range of changes inside and outside of the organization
2/ **Defining Change**	Defining the individual change the project is aiming to deliver	Defining the landscape into which changes are implemented and the journey from one change to the next	Defining the integrated map of changes that will deliver the organization's strategy
3/ **Managing Benefits**	Understanding and working with the benefits of a specific change	Understanding the benefits required from all past, current and future change and the combined effect of managing these	Actively managing an integrated benefits map that supports prioritisation and decision making across the organization
4/ **Stakeholder Strategy**	Identifying and engaging stakeholders involved in or impacted by a specific change	Identifying and engaging stakeholders involved in building and maintaining business wide processes and systems to enable change	Identifying and engaging internal and external stakeholders involved in setting direction and maintaining the organization's road map of change
5/ **Communication and Engagement**	Identifying and delivering the communication strategies, plans, activities and measures relating to a specific change	Managing and maintaining 'business as usual' communication skills, strategies, channels and measures	Managing and maintaining organization communication policy, standards, channels, feedback loops and measures internally and externally
6/ **Change Impact**	Identifying the impact of a specific change on the environment into which it is being delivered	Identifying and managing the cumulative impact of change on each role or department	Monitoring and managing change impacts of internal and external events across the organization

CMBoK Knowledge Area	Project	Business	Organization
7/ Change Readiness, Planning and Measurement	Developing and executing strategies and plans to build readiness for a specific change	Developing and executing strategies and plans to build ongoing change readiness in the people and environment receiving change	Developing and executing strategies and plans to set standards and develop change readiness required to deliver future business strategies and plans
8/ Project Management	Working as part of a project	Playing an active and effective role in projects	Actively managing the organization's strategy and road-map of change to guide project governance
9/ Education and Learning Support	Analysing skills gaps and developing training and support strategies and plans to support a specific change	Developing and maintaining learning and support channels, enabling capacity for learning, building general skills and setting standards	Providing and maintaining organization-wide standards, partnerships, policies and channels for learning and support
10/ Facilitation	Facilitating a process or event in relation to a specific change	Creating an environment where consultation is valued and effective	Providing the frameworks, skills and facilities for effective internal and external group engagement
11/ Sustaining Systems	Ensuring all aspects of a specific change and the environment into which it is being implemented support the lasting effects required of that change	Maintaining awareness of the changes that are or will be embedded and managing their interdependencies. Monitoring and remediating change after implementation	Providing the culture, policies, frameworks and processes to support sustainable change across the organization
12/ Personal and Professional Management	Being a role model for people involved in or impacted by a specific change	Building and maintaining change leadership, emotional management and resilience in those receiving change	Building, role modelling, rewarding and maintaining high levels of self-awareness and self-management across the organization
13/ Organizational Considerations	Avoiding or leveraging organizational elements in support of a specific change	Prioritising and managing the cumulative effects of change on processes, policies, performance and structures	Providing and maintaining the organizational structures, IR, HR , IT and risk management policies to enable change

CPSIA information can be obtained at www.ICGtesting.com
Printed in the USA
LVIW01n1423260215
428489LV00011B/65